ALPHABET COOKING

From Angel-in-a-Cloud Cookies to Zebra Pudding Cups—
Fun Recipes for Children, from A to Z

ELAINE MAGEE, M.P.H., R.D.

CB
CONTEMPORARY BOOKS

Library of Congress Cataloging-in-Publication Data

Magee, Elaine.
    Alphabet cooking : from angel-in-a-cloud cookies to zebra pudding cups : fun recipes for children, from A to Z / Elaine Magee.
        p.   cm.
    Includes index.
    ISBN 0-8092-2970-6
    1. Cookery.   2. Cookery—Study and teaching.   3. Alphabet.
I. Title.
TX652.M237   1998
641.5—dc21   97-26731
                                                         CIP

Cover design by Monica Baziuk
Cover and interior illustrations by Lana Mullen
Interior design by Nancy Freeborn
Author photograph by Pickton's Photo/Graphics

Published by Contemporary Books
An imprint of NTC/Contemporary Publishing Group, Inc.
4255 West Touhy Avenue, Lincolnwood (Chicago), Illinois 60646-1975 U.S.A.
Copyright © 1997 by Elaine Moquette-Magee
Printed in the United States of America
International Standard Book Number: 0-8092-2970-6
18   17   16   15   14   13   12   11   10   9   8   7   6   5   4   3   2   1

This book is dedicated to Mrs. Berleth's kindergarten class (1996–97).
These twenty-two wonderful children brought this book to life.
Those eager and smiling faces, sparkling eyes, and welcoming hugs
made everything worthwhile.

Contents

Acknowledgments

I couldn't have had a more helpful and supportive teacher to test these activities with than Louise Berleth. A special thanks to my daughter, Devon, who was always happy to have her mom visit her kindergarten class, and to my youngest daughter, Lauren, who trooped along with me to every single alphabet cooking class.

Mrs. Berleth's kindergarten class (class of 1996–97)

Brittany Berg	Devon Magee
Katy Campbell	Simon Northall
Olivia Cole	Catherine Nuwer
Lauren Crawford	Lacey O'Brien
Alex Deane	Austin Parks
Kalvin Deng	Elizabeth Ruby
Patrick Dunphy	Mark Szymanski
Milaina Fraschieri	Jordan Tweddale
Kristin Fraser	Nicholas Victor
Adeline Gheorghita	Boaz Witbeck
Tucker Hacking	Megan Woodward

Introduction

Since I write cookbooks and a recipe column for a living, there isn't a day that goes by when my two daughters aren't in the kitchen with me eagerly offering to be tasters, stirrers, or egg crackers. As they get older, they start asking, "Mommy, can I do that?" That's why, to me, cooking with children is a natural and wonderful combination. I love the time we share together cooking. It seems I'm always learning something really important—like how my children think or feel, or maybe about something that happened that day at school.

There are certain cooking activities that have become family favorites—ones we do again and again. But I like to try new things with my girls, too. It's fun to incorporate things they might be learning in school, like historical events or favorite storybooks. That's how I got the idea to do an alphabet cookbook. Since children are learning the alphabet between ages three and six, why not reinforce the process with fun food activities? It sounded good to me. And it sounded good to the children in my daughter's kindergarten class.

Although the activities were written with the home kitchen in mind, I tested half of these food activities in my daughter's kindergarten class of twenty-two children. Consequently, many of these activities work well with larger groups. You will find any suggestions I might have to adapt activities to the classroom in the *Classroom Hints* section at the end of those activities.

Congratulations on buying this book. You have made a commitment to spend time together with your child doing something fun. Spending time with your child doing seemingly mundane activities like cooking should not be taken lightly. Time together is becoming a rare commodity in this day and age. And time spent cooking together is practically extinct. It doesn't have to be that way. Open up your heart, and open up your kitchen—this is the good stuff.

Set Up for Success

What's the point in cooking with your child if the time together is fraught with frustration and criticism? Just let go of your expectations for perfection. The end product may not look as nice as if you had made it by yourself, and the kitchen may not look as clean as if you alone were cooking, but that really wasn't the point anyway. The point is your child should feel proud of his or her efforts, and a little praise and support from you is going to help that along.

There are other little things you can do to help your child feel successful in the kitchen (see Minimize Mess, Spills, and Other Mishaps, below). Use good equipment such as Cushionaire or Roscho cookie sheets and thick, nonstick pots. The food project will be more likely to cook evenly and *not* burn.

Dress for Success

You may want to have a special apron for your child. He or she can wear an old shirt to protect clothes, come what may, such as flying food coloring. Canvas children's aprons can be bought at most craft stores for about three dollars. Buy some fabric paint or fabric markers to personalize your child's apron.

Dirty Dishes Are Part of Cooking

Teach your child that cleanup is part of cooking. When it's age appropriate, start involving him or her in as many cleanup jobs as you can. Start small. In preschool start your child washing his or her hands, throwing away garbage, and maybe even cleaning up the work area (when possible). By age seven (when your child can reach the sink), your child may even start to sponge off tables, wash and dry some dishes, fill the dishwasher, or put clean pots and pans away.

Minimize Mess, Spills, and Other Mishaps

You can set up your work area to minimize the mess, although some mess is inevitable. Here are a few suggestions:

- Have your child measure ingredients, from flour to milk, over a jelly roll pan. This way, whatever spills can simply be poured into the sink later.

- Use simple kitchen tools that make cooking easier. Egg separators are essential. Your child can separate the yolks from the whites one by one (catching the whites in a small bowl).

- Use standup (four-sided) graters. The one-sided versions are more difficult for little hands to manage.

- Use a plastic tablecloth to cover your kitchen table when painting cookies, making pizzas, rolling cookie dough, and so on. It makes for less stress during the activity (because the table is protected from spills) and easier cleanup.

- Create one cooking area where you concentrate most of your child's cooking, such as the kitchen table or one counter in your kitchen. This way, it won't feel like your entire kitchen is being ransacked. You will have one area to clean up instead of five different messes spread all over your kitchen.

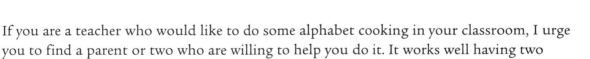

TIPS FOR THE CLASSROOM

If you are a teacher who would like to do some alphabet cooking in your classroom, I urge you to find a parent or two who are willing to help you do it. It works well having two adults involved, especially when the class size is twenty or more.

To adapt these activities for the classroom, you will need certain appliances, such as a nonstick electric skillet, a Crock-Pot, a blender, a bread machine, an ice-cream maker, a portable electric mixer—namely items that can be plugged in to available electric outlets in the classroom. You might want to make a list of the appliances you will need for the activities you have selected and circulate the list to parents, asking for volunteers to lend equipment on certain cooking days. One parent might contribute use of an electric skillet, while another will bring in a bread machine on bread day. You may even have parents donate spare or infrequently used appliances indefinitely.

It is a good idea to line up two of each appliance you need and to have the parents bring them in several days before they are actually needed, because I can guarantee some parents will forget to bring them in. You don't want to be stuck with a dozen eggs and no nonstick electric skillet to cook them in or with melting ice cream and no blender to froth it up in.

Here are some other helpful hints for the classroom.

Less is more. Keep in mind that the cooking activity will probably take more time than you think, so always opt in favor of doing less.

Expect the unexpected. Always have extra of everything—from paper cups, to marshmallows, to frosting.

The early and prepared bird catches the worm. Preheat your oven with plenty of time to spare (so you are not waiting for it during Cooking Time). Have all your equipment lined up and ready. Double-check what items you will need to bring from home. Generally, my rule of thumb is to bring just about everything from home; that way I know I will have it there. Pots and pans have a habit of disappearing from school kitchens from one week to the next, so it is hard to count on them for your purposes.

Provide all the comforts of home. Do as much preparation as you can at your own home. I've found that there are often other people using the school kitchen, so it is best for all concerned if you take up less time and space in the school kitchen.

Make the most of your captive audience. When your cooking class has a little downtime, perhaps as you are all waiting a few minutes for something to melt or boil, take advantage of it. This is when I usually take time to discuss a cooking technique or describe a chemical reaction that might be taking place. You can spell out the name of the recipe or foods being used on the chalkboard, and you can always have the children count the seconds if there is little time to wait until the next cooking step.

Last but not least, cleanup. Realistically, given time constraints, you (or a chosen parent) will most likely be the only one on the cleanup crew. Because you have so little time in the classroom with the children as it is, it is likely you will do the cleanup while the children are excused for recess. Still, this is an important component of cooking—one children need to be aware of. When time permits, have the children help with the cleanup. Remind them that while cooking and eating may be the fun part, cleaning up is the necessary part.

FOOD ACTIVITIES FROM

A TO Z

Applesauce-Oatmeal Cookies

EQUIPMENT

oven

cookie sheets

plastic knife

measuring cups and spoons

electric mixer and large mixing bowl

medium-sized bowl

mixing spoon

cookie scoop

spoon or spatula

wire racks

INGREDIENTS

6 tablespoons butter or margarine, softened

Canola oil nonstick cooking spray

½ cup applesauce

1 cup packed brown sugar

½ cup sugar

¼ cup low-fat buttermilk

¼ cup egg substitute

2 teaspoons vanilla extract

1 cup all-purpose flour

½ teaspoon baking soda

1½ teaspoons ground cinnamon

¼ teaspoon salt

3 cups old-fashioned oats

1 cup raisins

GROWN-UP PREP

1. Preheat oven to 350°F.
2. Coat cookie sheets with nonstick cooking spray.

A

1. Your child can count the 6 tablespoons on a stick of butter, cut them off tablespoon by tablespoon with a plastic knife, and put them in the large mixing bowl.

2. Your child can measure the applesauce and add it to the butter. Beat with mixer until blended.

3. Help your child measure the brown sugar and the sugar and add them to the butter mixture. Measure buttermilk, egg substitute, and vanilla and beat into butter mixture until light and fluffy.

4. Your child can measure the flour, baking soda, cinnamon, and salt and combine them in medium-sized bowl. Beat flour mixture into butter mixture.

5. Your child can measure the oats and raisins and stir them into the cookie dough.

6. Use cookie scoop to drop dough (or drop dough by rounded tablespoonfuls) onto prepared cookie sheets, leaving about 2 inches between cookies. For flatter cookies, your child will love to help you lightly press each cookie mound down with a spoon, spatula, or your fingers.

7. Bake in upper third of oven for about 10 minutes or until lightly browned. Cool the cookies on wire racks.

Makes 32 large cookies

Per cookie: 120 calories, 2 g protein, 22 g carbohydrate, 2.7 g fat, 1 g fiber, 5 mg cholesterol, 36 mg sodium; 20 percent of calories from fat.

CLASSROOM HINT

To make this activity go more smoothly, make a batch of the cookies at home ahead of time. Then during class time, the kids can help mix up a batch of cookie dough. Instead of waiting until the cookies bake in the school oven, you can bring out the cookies you already made!

Alphabet Chicken Soup

With luck, you will be able to find alphabet pasta. If you can't, use O-shaped salad macaroni noodles.

EQUIPMENT

stove

large nonstick saucepan

knife

can opener

measuring cups

measuring spoons

Crock-Pot

plastic knife

large nonstick frying pan

garlic press

CLASSROOM HINTS

Start the soup first thing in the morning. The class can smell the soup cook during the morning. The soup should be done in time for a prelunch snack! This recipe will yield about 14 4-ounce servings. Use a nonstick electric skillet preheated to 300°F instead of a frying pan and stove to cook the garlic, onion, and chicken.

INGREDIENTS

1½ cups dry alphabet pasta or salad macaroni noodles

Water

1 large onion

2 carrots

3 ribs celery

2 cooked boneless and skinless chicken breasts, *or* 1 10-ounce can white chicken meat in water

1 tablespoon butter or margarine

2 large garlic cloves

1 49-ounce can ⅓-less-salt chicken broth

2 teaspoons parsley flakes

Black pepper

1. Cook alphabet pasta or macaroni noodles according to directions on package in boiling water until tender, drain, and set aside. This will yield about 3 cups of cooked pasta.

2. Chop onion. (If Cooking Time is limited, slice carrots and celery also.)

3. Cut chicken into small chunks or open can of chicken and drain and rinse.

COOKING TIME

1. Your child can help you put the chicken broth into the Crock-Pot and turn it to high.

2. Your child can slice butter or margarine from a stick with a plastic knife and put in nonstick frying pan. Melt butter over medium heat and add the chopped onion. Your child can peel the skin away from the garlic cloves using a plastic knife and then use the garlic press. Add garlic to onions and cook until lightly browned, about 3 minutes.

3. Add chicken pieces and sauté a few minutes more. Add ⅓ cup of the chicken broth if the bottom is too dry.

4. You and your child can add chicken mixture to chicken broth in Crock-Pot, along with the carrots, celery, parsley flakes, pasta, and black pepper to taste. If you haven't already done so, your older child can help you slice the carrots and celery using an appropriate knife. Or your younger child can help wash the carrots and celery while you do the slicing. Cook soup until carrots are tender, about 2 hours.

Makes about / 8-ounce servings

Per 8-ounce serving: 176 calories, 14 g protein, 22 g carbohydrate, 4 g fat, 28 mg cholesterol, 152 mg sodium; 21 percent of calories from fat.

▶ Bread

EQUIPMENT

bread machine for 1½- or 2-pound
  bread loaves

measuring cups

measuring spoons

serrated knife

INGREDIENTS

1¼ cups water

1⅔ cups bread flour

1 cup all-purpose whole wheat flour

2½ teaspoons bread machine yeast

¼ cup packed brown sugar

2 tablespoons diet margarine or
  butter

1 cup old-fashioned oats

1¼ teaspoons salt

CLASSROOM HINTS

This activity works really well in the classroom. Have bread machine in the classroom and all the ingredients measured out and ready to go first thing in the morning. Use two bread machines to make two loaves if you have more than 15 students. You can get the bread machine started and then lead the children in making Butter. The Butter can be placed in the school refrigerator for a few hours until the Bread is ready. Then the children can eat their Bread with their homemade Butter. MMMM good!

1. Your child can help measure the ingredients and put them in the bread machine pan in the order recommended by the manufacturer. Explain to your child why each ingredient is added to make bread:

   ■ When mixed with a liquid and kneaded, flour makes an elastic dough that when baked forms the structure of bread.

   ■ The whole wheat flour is added to provide fiber and more vitamins and minerals.

   ■ The yeast is added to produce the gas that gives bread its air bubbles.

   ■ The sugar is added as food for the yeast.

   ■ The margarine is added for a moister crumb texture.

   ■ The oats are added for fiber and flavor.

   ■ The salt is added to control the yeast activity and for flavor.

2. Set the bread machine to the whole wheat or basic/white cycle using medium crust setting. Your child can push START. When bread has finished (about 4 hours 20 minutes), remove it from pan. Use a serrated knife to cut the bread into slices, and serve it with the butter from the next activity.

One loaf makes 12 slices

Per slice: 136 calories, 5 g protein, 26 g carbohydrate, 1.7 g fat, 2.5 g fiber, 0 mg cholesterol, 233 mg sodium; 11 percent of calories from fat.

▶ Butter

EQUIPMENT

2-quart jar with tight lid and marble
   or baby food jars

strainer

2-quart bowl

wooden spoon

serving bowl

INGREDIENTS

2 to 4 cups heavy whipping cream,
   chilled well

⅛ teaspoon salt

GROWN-UP PREP

Chill the large jar and marble or baby food jars in the refrigerator for at least 1
hour; it helps the butter form quickly. Place the strainer over the bowl.

CLASSROOM HINTS

*Use one baby food jar for each
student. Four cups of cream
will fill 32 baby food jars.
If you use the 2-quart jar, pass
the jar around so every student
can take a turn shaking.*

COOKING TIME

1. If using the large jar, pour 2 cups of the cream into the jar, drop in the marble, and fasten the lid tightly. If using baby food jars, pour ⅛ cup of cream in each jar.

2. Lead your child in shaking the jar or jars. Continue shaking the jar or jars until the butter forms and separates from the buttermilk.

3. Your child can then pour the buttermilk and butter into the strainer.

4. After all the butter is strained, pour the buttermilk from the bowl into another large jar (the buttermilk can be used for another cooking activity).

5. Your child can help you wash the butter with water in the strainer until the water runs clear (you are washing out the remaining buttermilk). Wash the bowl out. Pour the butter chunks from the strainer into the bowl. Use the wooden spoon to stir and press the butter against the side of the bowl to work out any remaining buttermilk. Your child will love to help you do this. Pour the buttermilk off.

6. Your child can put the butter chunks in the serving bowl and stir in the salt. Chill in refrigerator or keep over ice until needed.

Makes about 1 cup of butter

Per teaspoon: 33 calories, 0 g protein, 0 g carbohydrate, 3.7 g fat, 0 g fiber, 10 mg cholesterol, approximately 28 mg sodium; 100 percent of calories from fat.

Carrot Cupcakes with Cream Cheese Frosting

EQUIPMENT

oven

muffin pans

paper or foil muffin cups

egg separator

electric mixer and mixing bowl

bowl

spoon

measuring cups

measuring spoons

plastic knives

INGREDIENTS

Cupcakes

4 egg whites

1½ cups sugar

¼ cup vegetable oil

¼ cup corn syrup or maple syrup

1 8-ounce can crushed pineapple in juice

2 egg yolks

¼ cup egg substitute

2 cups all-purpose flour

2 teaspoons baking soda

3 teaspoons ground cinnamon

½ teaspoon ground cloves

1 teaspoon salt

6 carrots

Light Cream Cheese Frosting

¼ cup fat-free cream cheese

¼ cup light cream cheese

¼ cup diet margarine

¾ teaspoon vanilla extract

3½ cups powdered sugar

⅛ cup sprinkles, flaked coconut, or raisins (optional)

CLASSROOM HINT

If class time is limited, make the cupcakes ahead of time. Just make the cream cheese frosting with the kids, and they can frost the cupcakes in class.

GROWN-UP PREP

1. Preheat oven to 350°F.

COOKING TIME

1. Your child can line the muffin pans with paper or foil muffin cups.

2. Your child can help separate the egg whites from the yolks using an egg separator. Put egg whites in mixing bowl. Whip egg whites in mixing bowl until stiff. Spoon into another bowl and set aside.

3. Your child can measure the sugar, oil, syrup, and crushed pineapple and put them into the mixing bowl. Beat in the egg yolks and egg substitute.

4. Your child can measure the flour, baking soda, cinnamon, cloves, and salt and add them to the mixture. Beat mixture on low speed until blended.

5. Fold in the whipped egg whites. Your child can help grate and measure the carrots. Then stir them into the batter.

6. Fill muffin cups three-quarters full with batter. Bake 15 to 20 minutes or until center of cupcakes are firm and cupcakes are lightly browned.

7. While you are waiting for the cupcakes to bake, wash and dry the mixing bowl. Your child can measure the fat-free cream cheese and light cream cheese and put them in the mixing bowl. Your child can also measure the diet margarine and vanilla and add them to the cream cheeses.

8. Beat until smooth.

9. Meanwhile, your child can measure the powdered sugar and have it ready.

10. On low speed, beat in enough powdered sugar for desired consistency.

11. Your child can dip a plastic knife into the frosting to frost the cupcakes. Decorate cupcakes with sprinkles, flaked coconut, or raisins, if desired.

NOTE: I recommend using I Can't Believe It's Not Butter Light vegetable oil spread.

Makes 20 to 22 cupcakes

Per cupcake with frosting: 425 calories, 5 g protein, 85 g carbohydrate, 7.5 g fat, 1.5 g fiber, 35 mg cholesterol, 477 mg sodium; 15 percent of calories from fat.

Creepy Crawler Coleslaw

EQUIPMENT

shredder

knife

grater

electric mixer and mixing bowl

large resealable plastic bag

measuring cups

measuring spoons

INGREDIENTS

1 medium-sized head cabbage

2 carrots

⅓ cup sugar

½ teaspoon salt

⅛ teaspoon black pepper

¼ cup low-fat milk

½ cup low-fat mayonnaise

¼ cup low-fat buttermilk

1½ tablespoons distilled white vinegar

2½ tablespoons lemon juice

16 to 18 Gummy Worms

GROWN-UP PREP

1. Finely shred and chop cabbage. Place in large resealable plastic bag.

2. Grate carrots if Cooking Time is limited.

1. If time allows, have your child start grating carrots until 1 cup is collected.

2. Have your child measure the sugar and put it in mixing bowl.

3. Your child can measure the salt, pepper, milk, mayonnaise, buttermilk, vinegar, and lemon juice and add them to the sugar.

4. Beat mixture with electric mixer until smooth. Add cabbage and carrots and toss to blend.

5. Your child can add the Gummy Worms to the coleslaw.

Makes 16 to 18 ½-cup servings

Per ½-cup serving: 44 calories, 1 g protein, 9 g carbohydrate, .7 g fat, 1 g fiber, .5 mg cholesterol, 151 mg sodium; 14 percent of calories from fat.

CLASSROOM HINT

One of your students can count the Gummy Worms (one per child) and add them to the coleslaw.

Diggity Dogs

EQUIPMENT

oven

plastic knife

plates

cookie sheet

INGREDIENTS

1 8-ounce can Pillsbury reduced-fat
crescent roll dough

8 Ball Park Lite franks or Louis Rich
franks

8 slices reduced-fat American cheese,
cut in half (optional)

16 slices less-fat salami (optional)

CLASSROOM HINTS

*You can preheat the school
oven before Cooking Time.
Have each child prepare his or
her own Diggity Dog for
cooking. Then run them to the
oven. The Diggity Dogs make
a great school snack!*

GROWN-UP PREP

Preheat oven to 375°F.

COOKING TIME

1. Open can of crescent dough. Unroll the dough with your fingers into the individual dough servings. Have your child cut each rolled-out crescent dough triangle in half with a plastic knife to make two thinner triangles.

2. Have your child cut each of the hot dogs in half (to make two shorter hot dogs). Your child can lay the crescent roll triangle flat on a plate. Add cheese and/or salami, if desired. Place the hot dog at the base of the triangle. Roll each hot dog half with one of the crescent dough triangles starting at the base and ending with the tip of the triangle. Place about 2 inches apart on cookie sheet.

3. Bake for about 12 minutes or until rolls are lightly browned.

Makes 16 Diggity Dogs

Per 2 Diggity Dogs: 210 calories, 9 g protein, 16 g carbohydrate, 12.5 g fat, 0 g fiber, 20 mg cholesterol, 960 mg sodium; 53 percent of calories from fat.

Dip and Dippers

d

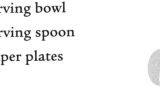

EQUIPMENT

vegetable peeler

vegetable scrub brush

knife

serving tray

serving bowl

serving spoon

paper plates

d

INGREDIENTS

16 ounces fat-free sour cream

2 tablespoons mayonnaise

1 1-ounce envelope Hidden Valley Ranch Original Ranch Party Dip mix, Lipton Recipe Secrets onion recipe soup mix, or Hidden Valley bacon and onion ranch dips mix

Assorted vegetables, such as 1 small jicama, 2 to 3 carrots, 2 to 3 ribs celery, 1 zucchini, and 6 cherry tomatoes

2 cups reduced-fat potato chips (optional)

2 cups reduced-fat crackers (optional)

CLASSROOM HINTS

Make two dips and set up a buffet table with the dips and all the dippers you have selected and prepared. The children can form a line and go through the buffet adding the dips and dippers to their plates.

GROWN-UP PREP

1. If Cooking Time is limited, peel, cut, and wash (as needed) the vegetables you will be using. Arrange them on a serving tray.

COOKING TIME

1. Your child can help you wash, peel, and cut (if age appropriate) the various vegetable dippers you have chosen.

2. Your child can dump the sour cream and mayonnaise into the serving bowl.

3. Your child can tear the envelope of dip mix open and pour it over the sour cream mixture.

4. Using a serving spoon, your child can stir the dip until all the ingredients are blended well.

5. Your child can spoon some dip onto his or her plate along with an assortment of veggie dippers and potato chips and crackers, if desired.

NOTE: I buy Naturally Yours fat-free sour cream in the cowhide-colored container.

Makes 16 servings

Per ⅛ cup of dip and ½ cup of assorted vegetable dippers: 53 calories, 2.5 g protein, 7.5 g carbohydrate, 1.5 g fat, .6 mg cholesterol, 300 mg sodium; 25 percent of calories from fat.

Elephant Cookies

This activity works well with Frosting activity (see Index).

EQUIPMENT

measuring cups

measuring spoons

medium-sized bowl

electric mixer and mixing bowl

plastic wrap

oven

spatula

cookie sheets

rolling pin

elephant cookie cutter

wire racks

INGREDIENTS

3 cups all-purpose flour

2 teaspoons ground cinnamon

¾ teaspoon salt

⅔ cup butter, softened

⅓ cup fat-free cream cheese

1½ cups sugar

½ cup egg substitute

2 teaspoons vanilla extract

Canola oil nonstick cooking spray

About ½ cup powdered sugar

GROWN-UP PREP

Do the following between steps 4 and 5 of Cooking Time.

1. Preheat oven to 350°F.

2. Coat cookie sheets with nonstick cooking spray.

3. Dust dough, rolling pin, cookie cutter, and rolling surface with powdered sugar.

COOKING TIME

1. Your child can measure the flour, cinnamon, and salt and put them into the medium-sized bowl and stir to blend.

2. Your child can measure the butter, cream cheese, and sugar and put them into the mixing bowl. Beat until creamy.

3. Measure the egg substitute and vanilla and add to wet mixture. Beat until fluffy.

4. Beat dry mixture into the wet mixture on lowest speed of mixer, scraping sides. Divide dough in half and wrap each half with plastic. Refrigerate at least 1 hour (preferably overnight).

5. Your child can help you roll out half of the dough until it's ¼ inch thick. Press cookie cutter gently into dough. Pull cookie out of cutter and place on cookie sheet. Continue until you've used all the rolled-out dough. Add scraps to second half of dough, and repeat process.

6. Bake cookies in oven for 8 to 10 minutes or until just golden at the edges. Place cookies on wire racks to cool.

Makes 32 cookies

Per cookie: 117 calories, 2 g protein, 18.5 g carbohydrate, 4 g fat, 10 mg cholesterol, 96 mg sodium; 30 percent of calories from fat.

CLASSROOM HINTS

Make the cookies in advance to save time in the classroom since this activity is best paired with Frosting activity (see Index). Make the frosting with the class. Then the children can frost and decorate their cookies!

Extra-Cheesy Potato Skins

EQUIPMENT

nonstick frying pan

stove

small food processor or food
chopper

small serving bowl

fork

microwave oven

knife

cheese grater

medium-sized bowl or large
resealable plastic bag

oven

spoon

bowl

cookie sheet

measuring cups

medium-sized bowl

INGREDIENTS

Potato Skins

4 strips Louis Rich turkey bacon

4 russet potatoes

4 ounces reduced-fat sharp cheddar
cheese

Canola oil nonstick cooking spray

Low-Fat Ranch Dip (optional)

1 cup fat-free or light sour cream

1/8 cup low-fat mayonnaise

1/2 envelope Hidden Valley Ranch
Original Ranch Party Dip mix

GROWN-UP PREP

1. Cook turkey bacon in nonstick frying pan on medium-low heat, turning frequently, until crisp. Once it cools, chop bacon into small pieces in food processor. Keep in small serving bowl.

2. Pierce each potato a few times with fork. Microwave on HIGH for 10 minutes. Turn and rotate potatoes and cook on HIGH for another 10 minutes or until tender; cut potatoes in half lengthwise and set aside.

3. Grate cheddar cheese with cheese grater and store in medium-sized bowl or resealable plastic bag.

4. Preheat oven to 400°F.

COOKING TIME

1. Show your child how to scoop out about ½ inch from the center of each potato skin (half of a potato) using spoon. Have your child put aside extra potato in a bowl for making mashed potatoes later.

2. Show your child how to spray the skin side and the inside of the potato skins with nonstick cooking spray. Have your child place the sprayed potato skins on cookie sheet.

3. Your child can sprinkle ⅛ cup of grated cheese on each potato skin.

4. Your child can sprinkle about 1 teaspoon of bacon pieces over each top.

5. Bake in oven until cheese is bubbly and potato skins are just crisp, about 15 minutes.

6. While potato skins are baking, you and your child can make ranch dip, if desired. Mix sour cream, mayonnaise, and the dip mix in a medium-sized bowl. When potato skins have cooled, your child can add a dollop of ranch dip to each skin.

Makes 8 potato skins

Per potato skin: 170 calories, 8 g protein, 26 g carbohydrate, 3.5 g fat, 2.5 g fiber, 14 mg cholesterol, 280 mg sodium; 20 percent of calories from fat.

Frosting

EQUIPMENT

electric mixer and mixing bowl

measuring cups

4-cup measure

measuring spoons

spatula

INGREDIENTS

½ cup diet margarine

5 cups powdered sugar

⅛ teaspoon salt

3 tablespoons milk

1½ teaspoons vanilla extract

CLASSROOM HINTS

This activity works well with the Elephant Cookies. You can make the cookies ahead of time, whip up the frosting in class, and then the class can frost and decorate their elephant cookies!

COOKING TIME

1. Your child can measure the diet margarine and put it in a large mixing bowl.

2. Your child can measure powdered sugar and add it to diet margarine. You can fill a 4-cup measure (or 2 2-cup measures). Then ask your child how many more cups you need to make 5.

3. Add the salt to the powdered sugar, and your child can measure the milk and vanilla and add them to the bowl.

4. Blend all ingredients with mixer until smooth and creamy, scraping sides with spatula at least once.

NOTE: I Can't Believe It's Not Butter Light is a better tasting vegetable oil spread than most. But if you would rather not use diet margarine, blend ¼ cup of softened butter with ¼ cup of fat-free cream cheese instead of the ½ cup of diet margarine already called for.

Makes about 24 tablespoons of frosting

Per tablespoon of frosting: 98 calories, 1 g protein, 21 g carbohydrate, 2 g fat, 0 g fiber, .3 mg cholesterol, 30 mg sodium; 17 percent of calories from fat.

Fruit Punch

This is a super activity to do right before you are having a party or get-together.

EQUIPMENT

punch bowl and ladle

4-cup measure

INGREDIENTS

4 cups pineapple juice or bottled cherry juice

4 cups orange juice (pulp free if possible)

4 cups apple juice

4 cups diet lemon-lime soda or diet ginger ale

Ice cubes (optional)

COOKING TIME

1. Have your child measure pineapple juice, orange juice, apple juice, and soda and pour them into the punch bowl.

2. You or your child can stir the punch while the other is adding ingredients.

3. Your child can add ice cubes, if desired.

4. Guests can use the ladle to fill their cups with punch.

Makes 16 cups of punch

Per 1 cup of punch: 93 calories, .5 g protein, 23 g carbohydrate, 0 g fat, 0 mg cholesterol, 6 mg sodium; 0 percent of calories from fat.

Garden Salad

This dish includes a root (carrot), stem (celery), leaf (lettuce), flower (cauliflower or broccoli), fruit (apple cubes or raisins), and seed (sunflower seeds).

EQUIPMENT

knife

apple corer

serving bowls for each garden salad ingredient

bowls or plates

forks

INGREDIENTS

2 carrots

2 large ribs celery

8 cups romaine lettuce (or 1 head iceburg lettuce)

1 small bunch broccoli *or* ⅛ head cauliflower

2 apples

4 tablespoons sunflower seeds

Assorted salad dressings

COOKING TIME

1. You and your child have quite a few things to do:

   Wash and slice carrots thin (if age appropriate).

   Wash and slice celery thin (if age appropriate).

   Wash, drain, and tear lettuce into bite-sized pieces.

   Wash broccoli or cauliflower and break into florets.

   Core apples and cut into wedges, and then cut into cubes (if age appropriate).

2. Put each ingredient in a serving bowl. Set up a salad bar on an extra table in the kitchen. Place the salad dressings at the end of the salad bar.

3. Family members can go through the salad bar making their own garden salad. Encourage your child to try everything.

4. You may even have your child guess which of the salad bar ingredients is the root, stem, leaf, flower, fruit, and seed. Also mention that plant foods give us many good things that help us grow, like vitamins and minerals—so garden salads are a superhealthful food to eat.

NOTE: I think Wishbone olive oil vinaigrette is the best-tasting salad dressing of its kind.

Makes 8 salads

Per salad (not including dressing): 64 calories, 2.5 g protein, 9.5 g carbohydrate, 2.5 g fat, 2.5 g fiber, 0 mg cholesterol, 24 mg sodium; 32 percent of calories from fat.

CLASSROOM HINTS

Talk as a class about how things grow and that we eat many parts of plants. Prepare garden salad ingredients ahead of time if class time is limited. You'll need a bowl or plate and fork for each child.

Granola

EQUIPMENT

oven

10" × 15" baking pan

large mixing bowl

measuring cups

measuring spoons

4-cup measure (or medium-sized
bowl)

spoon

timer

INGREDIENTS

Canola oil nonstick cooking spray

¼ cup packed brown sugar

3 cups old-fashioned oats

1 cup white or whole wheat all-
purpose flour

½ cup wheat germ

½ cup sunflower seeds, pecan pieces,
or sliced almonds

¼ cup canola oil

¼ cup corn syrup or maple syrup

½ cup water or apple juice

1 tablespoon vanilla extract

½ teaspoon salt

1 cup sweetened shredded coconut

GROWN-UP PREP

1. Preheat oven to 275°F.

2. Coat baking pan generously with nonstick cooking spray.

COOKING TIME

1. Your child can measure the sugar, oats, flour, wheat germ, and sunflower seeds and put them into the large mixing bowl.

2. Your child can measure the oil, corn syrup, water, vanilla, and salt and put them into the 4-cup measure. Blend these ingredients well, and then drizzle over oats mixture. Toss to coat everything well.

3. Arrange Granola on prepared baking pan and bake 1 hour, stirring with spoon every 15 minutes. Have your child be in charge of the kitchen timer. He or she can set it for 15 minutes and let you know when the time is up.

4. Your child can measure the coconut and stir it into the Granola.

Makes about 7 cups

Per ½-cup serving: 227 calories, 6 g protein, 31 g carbohydrate, 9.5 g fat, 3 g fiber, 0 mg cholesterol, 99 mg sodium; 37 percent of calories from fat.

CLASSROOM HINT

Cook Granola in a nonstick electric skillet preheated to 275°F.

Hash Browns

This activity works well with the Omelet activity (see Index).

EQUIPMENT

potato peeler

grater or food processor

large nonstick skillet or saucepan
with lid

stove

measuring spoons

measuring cups

pancake turner

INGREDIENTS

5 potatoes

2 tablespoons canola oil

Canola oil nonstick cooking spray

Salt

Pepper

CLASSROOM HINT

You will need one nonstick electric skillet for the Omelet and one for the Hash Browns.

COOKING TIME

1. Help older children peel the potatoes with a potato peeler. With younger children, you may just want them to watch you do it; they can help by throwing away the peels as they come off.

2. Help your child coarsely grate the potatoes using the grater. Show him or her how to hold the potato safely. Or use the shredder attachment for your food processor if you prefer.

3. Heat skillet over medium heat. Pour in canola oil. When oil is hot, spread oil over surface of pan. Spread potatoes evenly in pan. Generously coat top with nonstick cooking spray. Cover and cook about 8 minutes.

4. Uncover and flip potatoes over with pancake turner. Sprinkle salt and pepper to taste over the top and continue cooking another 8 minutes or until potatoes are tender and browned.

Makes 5 servings

Per 1-cup serving: 193 calories, 3 g protein, 33.5 g carbohydrate, 5.5 g fat, 2.5 g fiber, 0 mg cholesterol, approximately 115 mg sodium; 26 percent of calories from fat.

▶ Harvest Bread

EQUIPMENT

resealable plastic bag

toy hammer or heavy jar

can opener

2-pound bread machine

measuring cups

measuring spoons

serrated knife

INGREDIENTS

1 tablespoon butter or margarine

$^2/_3$ cup pecan pieces

$^3/_4$ cup canned pumpkin

$^2/_3$ cup water

2 cups bread flour

1 cup all-purpose whole wheat flour

$^1/_4$ cup packed brown sugar

1$^1/_2$ teaspoons salt

1 teaspoon pumpkin pie spice

2 teaspoons bread machine yeast

GROWN-UP PREP

Soften or melt the butter.

COOKING TIME

1. Put the pecan pieces in small resealable plastic bag, and have your child hammer it with a toy hammer or the bottom of a heavy jar to break the pecans into smaller pieces.

2. Your child can help open the can of pumpkin with a can opener (if age appropriate), measure the pumpkin, and put it in the bread machine pan.

3. Your child can measure the water and butter and add them to the pumpkin.

4. Your child can measure the bread flour and whole wheat flour and add them to the pumpkin.

5. Your child can measure the brown sugar and add it.

6. Your child can measure the salt and pour it into one of the corners of the pan.

7. Your child can measure the pumpkin pie spice and add it.

8. Make a well in the flour and add the yeast.

9. Your child can pour the pecan pieces into the pan.

10. Press the basic/white cycle and medium or light crust on the bread machine, and then press Start.

11. After about 4 hours the bread will be ready. Remove baked bread from the pan. Use serrated knife to slice bread.

Makes 12 large slices

Per slice: 162 calories, 5 g protein, 26.5 g carbohydrate, 4.8 g fat, 2.5 g fiber, 0 mg cholesterol, 280 mg sodium; 26 percent of calories from fat.

Interesting Pizza Bread

EQUIPMENT

1½- or 2-pound bread machine

cheese grater

plastic knife

measuring cups

measuring spoons

serrated knife

INGREDIENTS

2 ounces part-skim mozzarella cheese or reduced-fat sharp cheddar cheese

⅔ cup turkey pepperoni slices

1 cup plus 2 tablespoons water

3 cups bread flour

2 tablespoons sugar

1½ teaspoons garlic salt

1½ teaspoons dried oregano leaves

2 teaspoons bread machine yeast

CLASSROOM HINTS

For a large class, cut each slice in half to make 24 half slices. Or run two bread machines at the same time so each student can have a whole slice.

1. Select basic/white cycle and medium or light crust on bread machine. Remove bread machine pan from bread machine.

2. Your child can grate the cheese.

3. Show your child how to cut the pepperoni slices into smaller pieces with plastic knife.

4. Your child can measure the water and put it in the bread machine pan.

5. Your child can measure the flour and add it to the water.

6. Your child can add the grated cheese and pepperoni pieces to the other ingredients.

7. Your child can measure the sugar and pour it into the pan.

8. Your child can measure the garlic salt and pour it into one of the corners of the pan.

9. Your child can measure the oregano and add it to the other ingredients.

10. Make a well in the center of the flour. Measure the yeast and pour it into the center of the flour.

11. Your child can press Start. Your child can watch the machine mix the ingredients into a dough within the first 5 minutes.

12. After about 4 hours and 20 minutes (depending on the bread machine), the bread will be hot and ready. Remove bread from pan and slice.

Makes 12 large slices

Per slice: 135 calories, 6.5 g protein, 23 g carbohydrate, 2 g fat, 1 g fiber, 9 mg cholesterol, 250 mg sodium; 12 percent of calories from fat.

Italian Breadsticks

EQUIPMENT

measuring cups

measuring spoons

1½- to 2-pound bread machine

oven

plastic knife

small microwave-safe cup

garlic press

microwave oven

pastry brush

2 cookie sheets

INGREDIENTS

1¼ cups water

1½ tablespoons olive oil

1½ teaspoons sugar

2 teaspoons salt

6 tablespoons cornmeal

3 cups all-purpose unbleached
    white flour plus extra

1 tablespoon yeast

1½ tablespoons butter

2 garlic cloves

i

1. Measure the water, olive oil, sugar, salt, cornmeal, flour, and yeast and put them into the bread machine pan in the order recommended by the manufacturer.

2. Set bread machine to dough cycle and press Start. After approximately 1 hour and 40 minutes your breadstick dough will be ready.

3. Preheat oven to 425°F.

COOKING TIME

1. Your child can measure and cut the butter from a stick using the plastic knife and put it into small microwave-safe cup. Your child can press the garlic cloves using a garlic press and add the garlic to the butter. Cook in microwave oven on HIGH for 20 seconds or so to melt butter. Set aside until needed.

2. Divide breadstick dough in half and divide each half into 6 pieces to make 12 pieces altogether. You and your child can roll each piece on a well-floured surface to coat well with flour. Then you and your child can roll the dough in between your palms to make a rope about 12 inches long.

3. Set breadsticks on cookie sheets, about 6 per cookie sheet. Dip pastry brush in butter mixture and brush over breadsticks.

4. Bake about 10 minutes or until lightly browned.

Makes 12 breadsticks

Per breadstick: 162 calories, 4 g protein, 28 g carbohydrate, 3.5 g fat, 1.5 g fiber, 4 mg cholesterol, 371 mg sodium; 20 percent of calories from fat.

Jam

EQUIPMENT

plastic knife

nonstick electric skillet

large bowl (clear if possible)

pastry blender or potato masher

measuring cups

medium-sized bowl

2-cup measure or small bowl

wooden spoon

ladle

glass jars

INGREDIENTS

1 pound fresh strawberries

1 pound fresh or frozen
   boysenberries or raspberries

4 cups sugar

1.75-ounce box Sure-Jell for lower-
   sugar recipes

1½ teaspoons butter or margarine

GROWN-UP PREP

Thaw boysenberries or raspberries slightly if frozen.

COOKING TIME

1. Your child can help you wash strawberries well and then pull off their stems. You and your child can slice the strawberries with a plastic knife.

2. Plug in electric skillet and heat to 400°F.

3. Put sliced strawberries and boysenberries or raspberries in large bowl.

4. Your child can help mash the berries using a pastry blender or potato masher.

5. Your child can help measure the sugar and put it in the medium-sized bowl.

6. Your child can scoop ¼ cup of the sugar from the bowl and put it in 2-cup measure or small bowl. Add the Sure-Jell powder to this sugar and mix well with wooden spoon.

7. Add the Sure-Jell mixture to the mashed fruit; your child can stir well.

8. Your child can slice butter from a stick with plastic knife and add to fruit mixture. The butter prevents foaming.

9. Pour fruit mixture into electric skillet and begin cooking. Bring mixture to a full rolling boil, in which the boiling doesn't stop when mixture is stirred; stir constantly.

10. Quickly stir in the rest of the sugar. Return mixture to full rolling boil and continue to boil, stirring constantly, for a few more minutes. Turn skillet off.

11. Ladle jam into jars. Make labels, if desired. Give some jars to neighbors, friends, or family members. Keep all jars in refrigerator.

NOTE: Jam will keep for up to 1 month.

Makes about 6 cups of jam

Per 1 tablespoon of jam: 36 calories, 0 g protein, 9 g carbohydrate, .2 g fat, <1 g fiber, <1 mg cholesterol, 2 mg sodium; 5 percent of calories from fat.

CLASSROOM HINTS

If classroom time is limited, slice strawberries before class. Once jam is reasonably cool, pour ¼ cup (for 24 students) or ½ cup (for 12 students) of jam into individual cups. The children can take the jam home to share with their families!

Jelly-and-Peanut-Butter Bars

This is a great activity to do at home!

EQUIPMENT

oven

9" × 13" × 2" baking pan

plastic knife

small microwave-safe bowl

measuring spoons

microwave oven

measuring cups

electric mixer and mixing bowl

spoon

INGREDIENTS

Canola oil nonstick cooking spray

2 tablespoons butter or margarine

6 tablespoons reduced-fat peanut
butter

1 517-gram Betty Crocker
SuperMoist French vanilla cake
mix

½ cup egg substitute

1 cup reduced-sugar jelly of any
flavor

GROWN-UP PREP

Preheat oven to 375°F.

COOKING TIME

1. Your child can spray the bottom and sides of baking pan with nonstick cooking spray.

2. Your child can cut 2 tablespoons of butter with plastic knife and place it in small microwave-safe bowl. Your child can measure peanut butter and add it to the butter. Microwave on defrost setting for 1 to 2 minutes (until butter has melted and peanut butter is soft). Put mixture in mixing bowl.

3. Pour cake mix into the mixing bowl.

4. Your child can measure the egg substitute and add it to the peanut butter.

5. Blend ingredients on low speed of mixer until dough forms. You may have to stir the mixture by hand a bit to incorporate all the loose crumbs. Spoon the dough into the prepared baking pan. Using his or her hands (washed and dried, of course), your child can press dough to evenly cover bottom of pan.

6. Your child can spread jelly evenly over the dough in pan to within ½ inch of edges using spoon. Bake 20 minutes or until just golden brown around edges. Cool completely. Cut into bars.

Makes 24 bars

Per bar: 157 calories, 3 g protein, 26 g carbohydrate, 4 g fat, 1 g fiber, 0 mg cholesterol, 200 mg sodium; 24 percent of calories from fat.

Ketchup

This activity works well with Diggity Dogs (see Index).

EQUIPMENT

can opener

food processor or blender

measuring spoons

spatula

INGREDIENTS

1 15-ounce can tomato puree

2 tablespoons vinegar

3 tablespoons Wondra quick-mixing flour

2 tablespoons sugar

1 teaspoon onion powder

$\frac{1}{4}$ teaspoon white pepper

$\frac{1}{4}$ teaspoon celery salt

$\frac{1}{16}$ teaspoon ground cloves

$\frac{1}{8}$ teaspoon ground cinnamon

$\frac{1}{8}$ teaspoon ground red pepper or chili powder

5 drops red food coloring (optional)

CLASSROOM HINT

You might want to have another adult baking french fries while the class is making the Ketchup.

COOKING TIME

1. Have your older child open the can of tomato puree. Pour into food processor.

2. Your child can measure the vinegar and pour it into the food processor.

3. Your child can measure the flour and sugar and add them to the tomato puree.

4. Your child can measure the onion powder, white pepper, celery salt, cloves, cinnamon, and red pepper and add them to the tomato puree.

5. Your child can count drops of food coloring into the food processor, if desired (it creates a more vividly colored Ketchup).

6. Process ingredients about 5 seconds. Scrape sides with spatula and process another 5 seconds. Serve with french fries (see Note).

NOTE: If you are going to serve the Ketchup with french fries, you'll need to bake the french fries before Cooking Time. I suggest using Oreida Country Fries, which are lower in fat than many other frozen french fries and taste great. Prepare according to manufacturer directions. The french fries should be cool enough to eat by the time the Ketchup is made.

Makes about 16 tablespoons

Per 1 tablespoon: 23 calories, .6 g protein, 5.5 g carbohydrate, 0 g fat, .7 g fiber, 0 mg cholesterol, 122 mg sodium; 2 percent of calories from fat.

Kiwi Kabobs

EQUIPMENT

5 serving bowls
melon ball tool (optional)
bamboo skewers
paper plates

INGREDIENTS PER SERVING:

½ kiwi, sliced in quarters
¼ cup banana slices
⅛ cup seedless grapes
¼ cup watermelon balls or cubes
2 large marshmallows

CLASSROOM HINTS

Once the students have gone through the kabob assembly line, they can put their kabobs on plates and sit down at their seats to enjoy them. If you don't want to do the kabob assembly line, place enough ingredients to make one kabob on each plate. Then the children can thread the ingredients onto their bamboo skewers at their seats.

GROWN-UP PREP

1. Put kiwi quarters, banana slices, grapes, watermelon balls, and marshmallows into separate serving bowls.

2. Make a kabob assembly line on a table in the kitchen. Set the bamboo skewers at the beginning of the line, followed by the serving bowls filled with kabob ingredients, followed by the paper plates.

COOKING TIME

1. Demonstrate for your child how to thread the various kabob ingredients onto the bamboo skewer, for example: put on the skewer a banana slice, then a grape, then a kiwi quarter, then a marshmallow, then a watermelon ball, and so forth.

2. Have your child go through the kabob assembly line, making many kabobs. Serve them at a weekend barbecue, party, or church social.

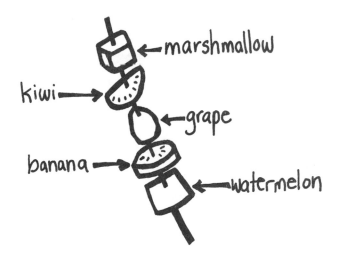

NOTE: Other fruits can be substituted for any of those listed in Ingredients.

Per kabob: 129 calories, 1.5 g protein, 32 g carbohydrate, .6 g fat, 2 g fiber, 0 mg cholesterol, 10 mg sodium; 4 percent of calories from fat.

Lollipops

EQUIPMENT

measuring cups

2 small microwave-safe bowls *or*
   2 2-cup glass measuring cups

microwave oven

several small shallow dishes

pretzel rod candy molds (optional)

waxed paper

INGREDIENTS

1 cup white chocolate chips

1 cup semisweet chocolate or milk
   chocolate chips

16 large pretzel rods

Assorted decorations, about ⅛ cup
   each, such as rainbow sprinkles
   or other small cake decorations
   or gumdrops, jelly beans, M&M's,
   or other candies

GROWN-UP PREP

Fill small shallow dishes with the decorations.

COOKING TIME

1. Your child can measure the white chocolate chips and put them in a small microwave-safe bowl. Heat in microwave on HIGH, stirring after each 30 seconds, until melted (about 2 minutes). Set aside.

2. Your child can measure the semisweet chocolate or milk chocolate chips and put them in a second small microwave-safe bowl. Heat in microwave on HIGH, stirring after each 30 seconds, until melted (about 2 minutes).

3. You and your child can dip each pretzel rod in either the melted chocolate or the melted white chocolate. Tilt the bowls to coat as much of the pretzel rods as possible.

4. Your child can roll the dipped rods in decorations or shake decorations over them. Place rods on waxed paper to harden.

Makes 16 chocolate-dipped pretzel lollipops

Per lollipop: approximately 108 calories, 2 g protein, 18.5 g carbohydrate, 3.7 g fat, 1 g fiber, 0 mg cholesterol, 180 mg sodium; 29 percent of calories from fat.

▶ Lemonade-in-a-Cup

EQUIPMENT

knife

cups

spoons

measuring spoons

measuring cups

INGREDIENTS

10 lemons (preferably soft-skinned lemons such as Meyer)

10 tablespoons sugar plus extra sugar

7 cups cold water

Ice cubes (optional)

CLASSROOM HINTS

Put a lemon half, a cup, and a spoon at every child's seat in the classroom. Then set up a lemonade table in the classroom with a serving bowl of sugar, a pitcher of cold water, and a bucket of ice if desired. The children can come up to the table in groups of four or five to add their sugar, water, and ice.

GROWN-UP PREP

Cut all the lemons in half.

COOKING TIME

1. Demonstrate for your child how to squeeze the lemon half so the juice falls into a cup. Show your child how to remove any seeds with a spoon.

2. Show your child how to add 1½ teaspoons of the sugar and then ⅓ cup of the cold water to each cup.

3. Your child can stir the Lemonade using a spoon. Add ice, if desired.

½ lemon → ← 1½ tsp. sugar

ice ← → water

NOTE: You and your child can make a pitcher of lemonade by squeezing the juice from lemon halves into a large pitcher. Measure and add sugar and cold water and stir.

Makes ½ cup of lemonade for each half lemon

Per ½-cup serving: 33 calories, .3 g protein, 9 g carbohydrate, 0 g fat, .5 g fiber, 0 mg cholesterol, .6 mg sodium; 2 percent of calories from fat.

Melon Moon Salad

EQUIPMENT

long, sharp knife

large spoon

plastic knife

large serving bowl

melon ball tool

INGREDIENTS

1 large cantaloupe

½ large seedless watermelon *or*
    1 small seedless watermelon

Casaba or honeydew melon

1. Cut cantaloupe in half. Your child can help scoop out the seeds with a large spoon. Slice each half into many thin wedges (sideways these should resemble crescent moons). Your child can remove the peel of each cantaloupe wedge with a plastic knife. Put in large serving bowl.

2. Demonstrate for your child how to make a watermelon ball using the melon ball tool. Your child can try his or her hand at making melon balls. Add all to the cantaloupe.

3. Cut the casaba or honeydew melon in half; remove the seeds with a large spoon. Make melon balls and then cut each ball in half with a plastic knife; add to other melon.

4. Mix the melon in the bowl. Talk about how you have three moon shapes in the salad: a crescent moon (the cantaloupe), a half moon (the casaba or honeydew melon), and a full moon (the watermelon).

Makes 10 servings

Per 1-cup serving: 154 calories, 4 g protein, 36 g carbohydrate, 1.6 g fat, 2.4 g fiber, 0 mg cholesterol, 30 mg sodium; 8 percent of calories from fat.

Marshmallow Clowns

EQUIPMENT

plastic knife

INGREDIENTS

1 marshmallow per serving

SnackWell's vanilla and/or chocolate frosting

1 reduced-fat vanilla or chocolate wafer per serving

1 chocolate kiss per serving

Decorator's writing gel

CLASSROOM HINTS

On a table in the classroom arrange all the clown ingredients. Each child can take a paper plate and pick up one of each of the clown ingredients, including a spoonful of frosting. Direct the children on assembling their clowns at their desks.

COOKING TIME

1. Show your child how to make a Marshmallow Clown by first taking a marshmallow and spreading a little bit of frosting on both flat ends with plastic knife. Press one flat end of the marshmallow on the rounded side of a wafer cookie. Then press a chocolate kiss down on the other frosted end of the marshmallow.

2. Your child can decorate each clown by making a face, a collar, and so forth using the writing gel and any other decorations you want to make available.

NOTE: Decorator's writing gel comes in assorted colors. You will find it in the cake decoration section of your supermarket. You may use other decorator's tubes. Hershey's Hugs may be substituted for kisses; their swirled colors look very cute.

Per clown: approximately 90 calories, .7 g protein, 16 g carbohydrate, 3 g fat, 0 g fiber, 3 mg cholesterol, 42 mg sodium; 29 percent of calories from fat.

No-Bake Chocolate Chews

EQUIPMENT

large saucepan

stove

large wooden spoon

measuring spoons

measuring cups

2 small spoons

2 to 3 mini muffin pans (with 12 mini muffin cups each)

INGREDIENTS

1½ cups sugar

¼ cup unsweetened cocoa

4 tablespoons butter

¼ cup light corn syrup

½ cup milk

⅛ teaspoon salt

½ cup reduced-fat peanut butter

1½ teaspoons vanilla extract

2 cups old-fashioned oats

2 cups crisped rice cereal

GROWN-UP PREP

Combine sugar, cocoa, butter, corn syrup, milk, and salt in large saucepan. Bring to a boil. Boil for exactly 40 seconds, stirring constantly. Remove from heat. Stir in peanut butter with wooden spoon. Cool for about 30 minutes.

COOKING TIME

1. Your child can measure and stir the vanilla into the cooled chocolate mixture.

2. Your child can measure the oats and stir them into the mixture.

3. Your child can measure the crisped rice cereal and stir it into the mixture.

4. Your child can scoop about one tablespoon of the mixture with one spoon and use the other spoon to press it into a mini muffin cup. Repeat with all the batter. Put the muffin tins in the refrigerator for a couple of hours.

Makes 36 chews

Per chew: 97 calories, 1.8 g protein, 16.5 g carbohydrate, 3 g fat, 1 g fiber, 4 mg cholesterol, 62 mg sodium; 27 percent of calories from fat.

CLASSROOM HINTS

Make the chocolate mixture at home over the stove about 45 minutes before class. Then the mixture will be cooled just in time. You can bring the cocoa, butter, sugar, corn syrup, milk, and peanut butter to class to show the children how the chocolate mixture was made. If you have 18 or fewer children, have each of them press ⅛ cup of the mixture into a mini muffin cup. This will make 18 large chews.

▶ Nameplate Graham Snacks

EQUIPMENT

small serving bowls

paper plate

plastic knife

INGREDIENTS

1 graham cracker or low-fat graham cracker per serving

Creamy peanut butter or reduced-fat creamy peanut butter

SnackWell's vanilla frosting

Assorted toppings, such as chocolate chips, raisins, M&M's, and dried cranberries

Place toppings in small serving bowls.

COOKING TIME

1. Give your child a graham cracker on a paper plate.

2. Demonstrate for your child how to make a nameplate by spreading either peanut butter or frosting on the graham cracker with a plastic knife. Show your child how to write his or her name by sticking the toppings into the peanut butter or frosting.

NOTE: Children with longer names may need two graham crackers each.

Per nameplate (using 1 tablespoon of regular peanut butter and raisins): 175 calories, 5.3 g protein, 22 g carbohydrate, 9 g fat, 2 g fiber, 0 mg cholesterol, 115 mg sodium; 46 percent of calories from fat.

▶ Omelet

EQUIPMENT

cheese grater

storage-sized resealable plastic bag

electric mixer (or a fork) and mixing
bowl

measuring cups

nonstick electric skillet or large
nonstick frying pan

stove

spatula

INGREDIENTS

4 ounces reduced-fat sharp cheddar
and reduced-fat Monterey Jack
cheese

4 large eggs

1 cup egg substitute

¼ cup water

Canola oil nonstick cooking spray

CLASSROOM HINTS

*Coat electric nonstick skillet
generously with canola oil
nonstick cooking spray. Then
pour the entire egg mixture
into skillet heated to 350°F.
As eggs set, run a spatula
around the edge of the skillet,
lifting eggs and letting any
uncooked egg flow
underneath. When eggs are
almost set on top, sprinkle
some of the cheese across the
center of the omelet. Fold sides
over and cut into servings.*

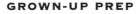

GROWN-UP PREP

Grate cheeses and keep in storage-sized resealable plastic bag

COOKING TIME

1. In mixing bowl, combine eggs (your child can crack them), egg substitute (your child can open the carton of egg substitute and pour it into mixing bowl), and water (your child can measure it and add it to eggs in mixing bowl). Beat egg mixture until just combined (not frothy).

2. Coat nonstick skillet generously with nonstick cooking spray.

3. Heat pan over medium heat. Pour half of egg mixture (about 1 cup) into heated skillet. As eggs set, run a spatula around the edge of the skillet, lifting eggs and letting any uncooked egg flow underneath.

4. When eggs are almost set on top, sprinkle half of the cheese across the center of the omelet. Fold in half and cut omelet into 2 servings.

5. Repeat process with remaining egg mixture and cheese. Don't forget to coat pan with nonstick cooking spray.

Makes 4 servings

Per serving: 184 calories, 21 g protein, 3 g carbohydrate, 9.5 g fat, 0 g fiber, 228 mg cholesterol, 313 mg sodium; 48 percent of calories from fat.

Operation Malted Milk Shake

EQUIPMENT

blender or food processor

measuring cups

measuring spoons

ice-cream scoop

child-sized mugs or cups

INGREDIENTS

2 scoops (1 cup) light vanilla ice cream

1½ tablespoons malted milk powder

¼ cup chocolate syrup

½ cup low-fat milk

GROWN-UP PREP

Set out the ice cream to soften 5 to 10 minutes before needed.

COOKING TIME

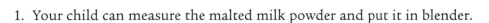

1. Your child can measure the malted milk powder and put it in blender.

2. Your child can measure the chocolate syrup and the milk and pour them into blender.

3. Use ice-cream scoop to scoop out 2 good-sized scoops of ice cream (at least 1 cup altogether); put ice cream in blender.

4. Put the top on and start blender. Pulse until blended well. Pour into 3 child-sized mugs or cups.

Makes 3 mini shakes

Per mini shake: 168 calories, 4.5 g protein, 30.5 g carbohydrate, 3.8 g fat, .5 g fiber, 25 mg cholesterol, 93 mg sodium; 20 percent of calories from fat.

Pancake Syrup

EQUIPMENT

nonstick electric skillet

1-cup measure

medium-sized bowl

measuring spoons

wooden spoon

gift jars or serving containers

INGREDIENTS

1 cup water

3 cups packed dark brown sugar

½ teaspoon ground cinnamon (optional)

2 teaspoons vanilla extract

COOKING TIME

1. Heat nonstick electric skillet to 400°F.

2. Your child can measure the water and pour it into the skillet. Wait for the water to boil.

3. While you are waiting for the water to boil, your child can measure the brown sugar and put it into medium-sized bowl. Your child can measure the cinnamon, if desired.

4. Once the water begins to boil, reduce heat to 300°F and add brown sugar (and cinnamon if desired). Stir constantly with wooden spoon until sugar is completely dissolved, about 5 minutes.

5. Your child can measure the vanilla and then pour it into the mixture. Pour the syrup into gift jars or serving containers.

Makes approximately 2⅓ cups

Per tablespoon: 83 calories, 0 g protein, 21 g carbohydrate, 0 g fat, 8 mg sodium; 0 percent of calories from fat.

CLASSROOM HINTS

If you would like the students to taste the Pancake Syrup with pancakes, you'll probably need to make them ahead of time. You'll need to make one pancake for every one or two children (depending on whether each child will have a whole pancake or a half of a pancake).

This is a terrific activity for the classroom. I made the pancakes at home, and then the class made the syrup using a nonstick electric skillet. I ladled each child a small spoonful of syrup onto a paper plate and gave each a pancake. The children loved it! You might decide to delete the cinnamon, though, in case some children in the class aren't fond of it.

Peanut Butter

EQUIPMENT

2-cup measure

food processor

measuring cups

measuring spoons

spatula

INGREDIENTS

1 pound roasted peanuts in their shells

⅛ cup diet margarine

⅛ cup light corn syrup

½ teaspoon salt

2 teaspoons molasses

⅛ cup water

CLASSROOM HINTS

Give each of the students some peanuts to shell. They can throw away the shells and add the peanuts to 2-cup measure. When you are running the food processor, have the children count to 60 twice as a way of passing the time. Serve each child a dollop of the peanut butter on a paper plate along with some celery and/or crackers.

1. Give your child some peanuts to shell. Throw the shells away, and your child can put the peanuts in 2-cup measure.

2. Put shelled peanuts in food processor.

3. Your child can measure the diet margarine and add it to the shelled peanuts.

4. Your child can measure the corn syrup and add it to the peanuts.

5. Your child can measure the salt and molasses and add them to the peanuts.

6. Process the peanut mixture until smooth. This may take a couple of minutes. If more moisture is needed (i.e., if some peanuts are drier than others), add water.

NOTE: I suggest you serve the Peanut Butter with reduced-fat Ritz crackers, celery sticks, or half slices of bread with assorted jellies (so your children can make their own peanut-butter-and-jelly sandwiches).

Makes 1½ cups (or 24 tablespoons)

Per tablespoon: 79 calories, 3 g protein, 3.5 g carbohydrate, 6.4 g fat, 1 g fiber, 0 mg cholesterol, 53 mg sodium; 68 percent of calories from fat.

Quilt Cookies

EQUIPMENT

measuring cups

measuring spoons

medium-sized bowl

mixing spoon

electric mixer and mixing bowl

rubber spatula

plastic wrap

oven

cookie sheets

rolling pin

plastic knife

bamboo skewers

wire racks

INGREDIENTS

3 cups all-purpose flour

2 teaspoons ground cinnamon

¾ teaspoon salt

⅔ cup butter, softened

⅓ cup fat-free cream cheese

1½ cups sugar

½ cup egg substitute

2 teaspoons vanilla extract

Canola oil nonstick cooking spray

1 cup powdered sugar

GROWN-UP PREP

Do the following between steps 4 and 5 of Cooking Time.

1. Preheat oven to 350°F.
2. Coat cookie sheets with nonstick cooking spray.
3. Dust dough, rolling pin, and work surface with powdered sugar.

COOKING TIME

1. Your child can measure the flour, cinnamon, and salt, put them in a medium-sized bowl, and stir to blend.

2. Your child can measure the butter, cream cheese, and sugar and put them in mixing bowl. Beat mixture until creamy.

3. Pour the egg substitute and vanilla into mixing bowl; beat until fluffy.

4. Beat the dry mixture into the wet mixture on lowest speed of mixer; scrape sides with spatula. Divide dough in half and wrap each half in plastic wrap. Refrigerate at least 1 hour, preferably overnight.

5. Your child can help you roll out half the dough to ¼ inch thick. Cut into rectangle-shaped cookies about 3 inches by 2½ inches with a plastic knife. Place cookies on prepared cookie sheets. Reroll scraps. Repeat with remaining dough.

CLASSROOM HINTS

Make the cookie dough ahead of time. Roll and shape the dough into cookies. Place on prepared cookie sheets. Bring these to class. Groups of 4 students can come up to the cooking table and "quilt" and "paint" their cookies. Then bake the cookies in the school oven and enjoy them as a snack.

6. You and your child can make quilt designs on each cookie by gently pressing the flat ends of the bamboo skewers into the tops of the cookies.

7. Bake cookies in oven for 8 to 10 minutes or until just golden at the edges. Cool cookies on wire racks.

NOTE: You and your child can paint the quilt cookies prior to baking. To make paint, mix about 10 drops of food coloring with about 2 teaspoons of water for each color. Dip paint brushes into the colors and paint your cookies.

Makes 24 cookies

Per cookie: 117 calories, 2 g protein, 18.5 g carbohydrate, 4 g fat, 10 mg cholesterol, 96 mg sodium; 30 percent of calories from fat.

Quick Muffins

EQUIPMENT

oven

muffin pans

foil or paper muffin cups

measuring cups

measuring spoons

electric mixer and mixing bowl

4-cup measure or another mixing
    bowl

large spoon

INGREDIENTS

Canola oil nonstick cooking spray

$\frac{1}{4}$ cup egg substitute

$\frac{1}{2}$ cup low-fat milk

1 tablespoon canola oil

3 tablespoons light corn syrup

1 teaspoon vanilla extract

$1\frac{1}{2}$ cups all-purpose flour

$\frac{1}{3}$ cup sugar

2 teaspoons baking powder

$\frac{1}{2}$ teaspoon salt

$\frac{1}{2}$ cup semisweet chocolate or milk
    chocolate chips

GROWN-UP PREP

Preheat oven to 400°F. Coat 12 muffin cups with nonstick cooking spray or line with foil or paper cups.

COOKING TIME

1. Have your child measure the egg substitute and pour it into mixing bowl. Your child can measure the milk, oil, corn syrup, and vanilla and add them to the egg substitute.

2. Beat mixture until blended.

3. Your child can measure the flour, sugar, baking powder, and salt and put them in 4-cup measure or a second mixing bowl. Your child can stir together with large spoon. Add flour mixture all at once to egg mixture. Stir just until moistened.

4. Your child can measure chocolate chips and add them to the batter.

5. Fill muffin cups ⅔ full with batter. Bake about 20 minutes or until lightly browned.

Makes 12 muffins

Per muffin: 144 calories, 3 g protein, 26.5 g carbohydrate, 3.5 g fat, 1 g fiber, 1 mg cholesterol, 191 mg sodium; 22 percent of calories from fat.

Raviolis

EQUIPMENT

food processor

pot sticker press or biscuit cutter with a press

measuring spoons

small bowl

large saucepan or stockpot

INGREDIENTS

10 slices Gallo light salami, chopped

1 cup part-skim ricotta cheese

⅓ cup grated Parmesan cheese

2 tablespoons egg substitute

1 teaspoon fines herbes or Italian seasoning

Black pepper

3 green onions, chopped fine (optional)

1 12-ounce package wonton wraps

Water

GROWN-UP PREP

Combine the salami, ricotta, Parmesan, egg substitute, fines herbes, black pepper to taste, and green onions, if desired, in food processor. Pulse until ingredients are blended well.

CLASSROOM HINTS

If time or cooking facilities are limited, you can make a batch of raviolis beforehand, boil them up, and spread them out on jelly roll pans. In class, you can demonstrate how to make raviolis using a couple of the wraps, some leftover filling, and the pot sticker press. Then the children can sample the ready-made raviolis.

COOKING TIME

Demonstrate for your child how to make a ravioli:

1. Lay one of the wraps on the pot sticker press.

2. Add 1 teaspoon of filling to the middle of the square.

3. Dip your finger in a small bowl of water and trace around the edges of the square.

4. Fold the square over to make a rectangular shape (with the cheese filling still in the center).

5. Use the pot sticker press to crimp the edges around the filling.

   Your child can try his or her hand at making raviolis. Boil the raviolis in saucepan or stockpot for 5 minutes and then serve.

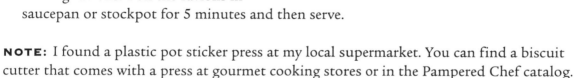

NOTE: I found a plastic pot sticker press at my local supermarket. You can find a biscuit cutter that comes with a press at gourmet cooking stores or in the Pampered Chef catalog. You can find wonton wraps in the produce section of your supermarket near the tofu.

Makes 50 raviolis

Per 2 raviolis: 65 calories, 3.5 g protein, 9 g carbohydrate, 2 g fat, 7 mg cholesterol, 144 mg sodium; 27 percent of calories from fat.

Raspberry Gelatin Cream

EQUIPMENT

saucepan

stove

measuring cups

medium-sized bowl

wooden spoon

ladle

serving bowls

INGREDIENTS

1 cup water to boil

1 3-ounce box raspberry gelatin

½ cup cold water

1 cup light vanilla ice cream

Miniature marshmallows (optional)

Light dessert topping, canned light
    whipped cream, or sweetened
    shredded coconut (optional)

GROWN-UP PREP

Start boiling water in saucepan. Once it boils, measure 1 cup and pour it into medium-sized bowl.

COOKING TIME

1. Your child can open the package of gelatin powder and pour it into boiled water. Your child can stir with wooden spoon until the gelatin is dissolved.

2. Your child can measure cold water and add it to the gelatin mixture, stirring until blended well. Let cool for 15 to 20 minutes. While you are waiting for the gelatin mixture to cool, set ice cream out to soften.

3. Your child can stir the ice cream into the gelatin mixture until melted. Stir in miniature marshmallows, if desired.

4. Pour or ladle gelatin mixture into 5 serving dishes. Refrigerate until firm, at least 2 hours. When ready to serve, add a dollop of light dessert topping, a squirt of canned light whipped cream, or a sprinkle of sweetened shredded coconut, if desired.

Makes 5 servings

Per ½-cup serving: 116 calories, 3 g protein, 22.5 g carbohydrate, 1.8 g fat, 14 mg cholesterol, 22 mg sodium; 14 percent of calories from fat.

▶ Strawberry Shortcake

EQUIPMENT

oven

wooden spoon

measuring cups

measuring spoons

large bowl

cutting board

rolling pin

3-inch biscuit cutter

cookie sheet

small mixing bowl

electric mixer

plastic knives

medium-sized serving bowl

INGREDIENTS

2⅓ cups Bisquick reduced-fat
   baking mix

½ cup low-fat milk

1 tablespoon canola oil

2 tablespoons corn syrup

Flour

Light dessert topping, canned
   whipped cream, or real whipped
   cream

½ cup powdered sugar plus extra
   (optional)

2 pints strawberries

GROWN-UP PREP

1. Preheat oven to 425°F. Stir Bisquick, milk, oil, and corn syrup together in
   large bowl until soft dough forms. Knead 8 or so times on lightly floured
   cutting board. Roll dough to ½ inch thick.

2. Cut out biscuits with 3-inch biscuit cutter. Place on ungreased cookie sheet.
   Bake 10 to 12 minutes or until golden brown.

COOKING TIME

1. While the shortcakes are baking, this is the perfect time for you and your child to prepare the whipped cream (if you are making it from scratch) and the strawberries. Your child can help you whip the whipped cream by first pouring the cream into the small mixing bowl. Beat with mixer. Once the cream is almost stiff enough, your child can sprinkle powdered sugar to taste into the bowl, if desired; blend well.

2. Your child can also wash the strawberries and help you prepare them by cutting out the green tops, and slicing the strawberries using a plastic knife.

3. Put strawberries in medium-sized serving bowl and sprinkle with powdered sugar to taste, if desired.

4. Split shortcakes with plastic knife. Your child can top each half with the sliced strawberries. Then top each half with a dollop of light dessert topping or whipped cream.

NOTE: You can make the biscuits ahead of time or your child can help you make those too—it's up to you.

Makes 6 servings

Per serving: 261 calories, 6 g protein, 47 g carbohydrate, 5.8 g fat, 3 g fiber, 1 mg cholesterol, 557 mg sodium; 20 percent of calories from fat.

(2 tablespoons of canned whipped cream adds 20 calories, 2 g fat, 1 g saturated fat, and 5 mg cholesterol to each serving.)

CLASSROOM HINT

Use a 2-inch biscuit cutter to make 10 mini shortcakes.

Snappy Sandwiches

EQUIPMENT

knife

biscuit cutter

heart-shaped cookie cutter

food processor

measuring spoons

measuring cups

cheese grater

spoon

plastic knives

INGREDIENTS

Roasted Chicken Spread

2 roasted chicken breasts, skinless and boneless

3 tablespoons low-fat mayonnaise

¼ cup nonfat cream cheese

Cheddar Cheese Spread

8 ounces reduced-fat sharp cheddar cheese

8 ounces nonfat cream cheese

9 slices special recipe white or whole wheat or cracked wheat bread

GROWN-UP PREP

1. Decide which spread you would like to make. If you would like to make roasted chicken spread, cut chicken into bite-sized pieces.

2. If Cooking Time is limited, cut some of the bread slices into interesting shapes, such as hearts or circles, ahead of time using biscuit or cookie cutter. Press cookie cutter onto 1 slice of bread at a time. If bread doesn't cut all the way, use a plastic knife to cut around the cookie cutter. Set aside some whole slices to use to make triangular sandwiches.

COOKING TIME

To make roasted chicken spread:

1. Put chicken pieces in food processor.

2. Your child can measure the mayonnaise and add it to the chicken.

3. Your child can measure the cream cheese and add it to the chicken.

4. Pulse food processor until ingredients are blended well and are spreadable.

To make cheddar cheese spread:

1. Your child can grate the cheese. Put grated cheese in food processor.

2. Your child can spoon the cream cheese from its container into the food processor.

3. Pulse food processor until ingredients are blended well and are spreadable.

4. Show your child how to make a double-layered sandwich:

   Spread some of the roasted chicken or cheddar cheese spread on two slices of bread of the same shape, whether heart-shaped, round, or whole slice.

   Cover one of the slices with a third slice of bread of the same shape.

   Top that slice with the spread side of the second slice of bread.

   To make 4 triangular sandwiches from double-layered sandwiches made from whole slices, cut the sandwich diagonally one way and then the other. You may need to do this with a serrated knife.

5. Repeat with other whole slices of bread or bread cut into hearts or circles.

NOTE: I like to use leftover BBQ chicken breasts for the chicken spread.

One spread recipe makes about 12 heart-shaped, round, or triangular mini sandwiches

Per 3 roasted chicken spread mini sandwiches (approximately): 259 calories, 21 g protein, 31 g carbohydrate, 3.5 g fiber, 40 mg cholesterol, 474 mg sodium; 21 percent of calories from fat.

Per 3 cheddar cheese spread mini sandwiches (approximately): 356 calories, 29 g protein, 33 g carbohydrate, 12 g fat, 3.5 g fiber, 35 mg cholesterol, 870 mg sodium; 30 percent of calories from fat.

▶ Tortillas

EQUIPMENT

large mixing bowl
pastry blender
kitchen towel
rolling pin
stove
nonstick frying pan

INGREDIENTS

1¼ cups all-purpose unbleached
    flour, plus extra

¼ cup diet margarine

½ cup plus 2 tablespoons warm
    water

Canola oil nonstick cooking spray

1½ to 2 cups grated reduced-fat
    Monterey Jack or sharp cheddar
    cheese (optional)

CLASSROOM HINT

*Use a nonstick electric skillet
preheated to 350°F instead of
a nonstick frying pan. Preheat
nonstick electric skillet about
5 minutes before you need to
use it.*

GROWN-UP PREP

1. Place 1¼ cups flour in a large mixing bowl. Combine the diet margarine with the flour with a pastry blender until it is cut up into pea-sized pieces. Stir in water. Mix into a dough.

2. Divide into 12 balls. Cover with dish towel and set aside for 20 minutes.

COOKING TIME

1. Prepare a floured surface. With your child's help roll each ball into a 5½-inch circle with rolling pin.

2. Spray nonstick frying pan or skillet with nonstick cooking spray. Cook tortillas one or two at a time (if space permits) for one or two minutes on each side, until blisters appear and tortillas are lightly browned.

3. While the second side cooks, sprinkle grated cheese over the top, if desired.

Makes 12 tortillas

Per tortilla: 64 calories, 1.5 g protein, 10 g carbohydrate, 2 g fat, .5 g fiber, 0 mg cholesterol, 17 mg sodium; 28 percent of calories from fat.

Truffles

EQUIPMENT

small bowls

can opener

measuring cups

measuring spoons

electric mixer and mixing bowl

wooden spoon

stove

heavy 2-quart saucepan

INGREDIENTS

½ cup unsweetened cocoa *or* 1 cup sweetened shredded coconut

¾ cup fat-free sweetened condensed milk (not evaporated milk)

⅓ cup fat-free cream cheese

4 tablespoons unsweetened cocoa

9 ounces semisweet chocolate

2 teaspoons vanilla extract

⅛ teaspoon salt

½ cup reduced-fat chocolate wafer crumbs

GROWN-UP PREP

1. Put ½ cup cocoa or 1 cup coconut in small bowl; set aside.
2. Use can opener to open condensed milk and set aside.

COOKING TIME

1. In small bowl, blend cream cheese with 4 tablespoons cocoa until smooth using electric mixer; set aside.
2. In heavy saucepan over very low heat melt chocolate. With your supervision, your child can help stir the mixture using wooden spoon.
3. Add melted chocolate to cream cheese mixture and beat with mixer until smooth. Your child can measure the condensed milk and add it to the chocolate mixture. Your child can measure and add the vanilla, salt, and cookie crumbs; beat well to blend.
4. Refrigerate chocolate mixture in bowl for about 1 hour or until easy to shape.
5. Show your child how to shape the chocolate mixture into 1-inch balls. Roll each of the balls in cocoa or coconut.

Makes about 24 large Truffles

Per Truffle: 89 calories, 2 g protein, 14 g carbohydrate, 3.5 g fat, .5 mg cholesterol, 50 mg sodium; 25 percent of calories from fat.

► Upside-Down Ice-Cream Sundae

EQUIPMENT

microwave oven

plastic serving spoons

clear plastic tumblers

plastic spoons

ice-cream scoops

INGREDIENTS PER SERVING

½ cup light ice cream

1 tablespoon hot fudge or caramel
topping

1 maraschino cherry

1 teaspoon rainbow sprinkles or
chopped nuts

2 tablespoons light whipped cream

GROWN-UP PREP

1. Set out the ice cream 5 minutes before Cooking Time to soften.

2. Heat the hot fudge or caramel topping in microwave oven if necessary.

3. Set up your ice-cream sundae bar on a table in the kitchen. Arrange the items
   in backward order. Set out the cups first, then the cherries, the sprinkles or
   chopped nuts, then the whipped cream, then the hot fudge or caramel
   topping, and finally the ice cream and plastic spoons.

1. Ask your child in what order she would add the foods if she were going to make an ice-cream sundae. Then tell your child that today she will be doing everything backward—she is going to make an Upside-Down Ice-Cream Sundae.

2. Go through the ice-cream sundae bar showing your child how to make her own Upside-Down Ice-Cream Sundae. Mention that if there is something your child doesn't like, she doesn't have to add it to the sundae.

Per sundae: 195 calories, 4 g protein, 29 g carbohydrate, 6.5 g fat, 30 mg cholesterol, 60 mg sodium; 30 percent of calories from fat.

Unbelievably Easy Mini Eclairs

EQUIPMENT

measuring cups

measuring spoons

oven

large Cushionaire or Roscho cookie sheet

nonstick heavy, medium-sized saucepan

wooden spoon

electric mixer and mixing bowl

wire rack

plastic knife

spoon

INGREDIENTS

Canola oil nonstick cooking spray

SnackWell's chocolate frosting

¼ cup butter

¼ cup fat-free sour cream

1 cup water

⅛ teaspoon salt

1 cup all-purpose flour

2 large eggs

6 tablespoons egg substitute

Light dessert topping, canned light whipped cream, or real whipped cream

¼ cup powdered sugar

GROWN-UP PREP

Your older child can help you with prep by measuring the ingredients and stirring the dough.

1. Preheat oven to 400°F and coat cookie sheet with nonstick cooking spray. Set chocolate frosting out at room temperature to soften.

2. To make pastry, heat butter, sour cream, water, and salt in saucepan over medium heat until mixture boils and butter melts. Reduce heat to low and then pour all of the flour into the pan, stirring with wooden spoon very quickly to blend. Mixture should form a ball of dough.

3. Use wooden spoon to transfer ball of dough into mixing bowl and let cool 5 minutes. Add eggs one at a time, beating well after each addition. Add egg substitute, beating well.

COOKING TIME

1. Your child can help you drop dough into 12 mounds about 3 inches apart onto prepared cookie sheet. You and your child can mold each mound with a spoon into a 4-inch-long rectangle, piling up the dough as high as possible and rounding the ends.

2. Bake in oven until golden, about 25 to 30 minutes. Remove from oven and reduce temperature to 375°F.

3. Make a 1-inch-long slit on one side of each eclair (to help dry it out on the inside). Bake for 10 minutes longer, and then transfer to a wire rack to cool.

4. While the eclair shells are cooling, whip cream if necessary. Add powdered sugar once the cream is almost fully whipped.

5. You and your child can cut each eclair in half lengthwise with a plastic knife, leaving one side uncut (just like a hot dog bun). You and your child can fill each eclair in the middle with light dessert topping or whipped cream.

6. You and your child can spread 2 to 3 teaspoons of the chocolate frosting over each of the filled eclairs using spoon. Store in refrigerator until needed. Keeps well, covered, for 2 days.

NOTE: If you do not want to go to the extra effort of making the eclair pastry, use store-bought ladyfingers instead. With the same amount of whipped cream and frosting you will make at least 24 ladyfinger eclairs.

Makes 12 mini eclairs

Per mini eclair with light dessert topping: 98 calories, 3 g protein, 9.7 g carbohydrate, 5 g fat, .5 g fiber, 46 mg cholesterol, 90 mg sodium; 47 percent of calories from fat.

▶ Vegetable Lasagna

EQUIPMENT

small serving bowls

oven

aluminum tart pans

2 ⅓-cup measuring cups

INGREDIENTS PER SERVING

1 to 2 tablespoons thinly sliced zucchini

1 tablespoon sliced mushrooms

1 tablespoon grated carrot

1 tablespoon thawed chopped frozen spinach (optional)

1 teaspoon finely chopped green onion (optional)

⅓ cup bottled spaghetti sauce

3 wonton wraps

⅓ cup grated part-skim mozzarella or reduced-fat sharp cheddar cheese

GROWN-UP PREP

1. Set each vegetable topping in a serving bowl.

2. Set up an assembly line in the kitchen so that your child can walk through and put together the lasagna.

3. Preheat oven to 400°F.

COOKING TIME

Demonstrate for your child how to assemble the lasagna:

1. Pour some of the spaghetti sauce into the bottom of a tart pan.

2. Top with one of the wonton wraps.

3. Top that with more sauce, then vegetables, and then some of the grated cheese.

4. Top with another wonton wrap, more sauce, more vegetables, and some cheese.

5. Top that with another wonton wrap, any remaining sauce, and any remaining cheese.

6. Bake in 400°F oven for about 15 minutes.

NOTE: Use spaghetti sauce that has 4 grams of fat or less per ½-cup serving. Wonton wraps are square pasta wraps and can be found in your supermarket's produce section near the tofu.

Per serving: 232 calories, 14 g protein, 23.5 g carbohydrate, 9 g fat, 2 g fiber, 20 mg cholesterol, 729 mg sodium; 35 percent of calories from fat.

CLASSROOM HINTS

Write the name of each child on the bottom of the tart pans with a black marker. Send a couple of children at a time through the lasagna assembly line. It helps to have a couple of adults helping the children as they go through. After each child has finished putting his or her lasagna together, an adult can wrap it with foil. The kids can take them home. Their parents can bake the lasagnas for them at 400°F for about 15 minutes.

Very Berry Smoothie

EQUIPMENT

potato peeler

plastic knives

blender

measuring cups

measuring spoons

INGREDIENTS

⅔ cup light vanilla ice cream

1½ cups whole strawberries

1 6-ounce container low-fat
    boysenberry yogurt

2 to 4 tablespoons low-fat milk
    plus extra

CLASSROOM HINTS

Set a few students up washing, removing stems from, and slicing strawberries. You can make several batches of smoothie in the classroom with your blender. Just fill paper cups with ¼ to ½ cup of smoothie, so each student gets a smoothie sample!

Remove ice cream from freezer to soften 5 minutes or so before Cooking Time.

COOKING TIME

1. Your child can help you wash strawberries, scoop the green top portion off strawberries with potato peeler or plastic knife, and slice strawberries with plastic knife.
2. Your child can measure ice cream and put it in blender.
3. Your child can open the yogurt container and add it to ice cream.
4. Your child can measure the milk and add it to ice cream (you can add a tablespoon or two more later if needed).
5. Measure sliced strawberries and add to ice cream.
6. Blend until mixture is smooth. Add 1 to 2 tablespoons milk if needed.

Makes about 2 cups of smoothie

Per 1-cup serving: 185 calories, 6.7 g protein, 33 g carbohydrate, 3.5 g fat, 1.5 g fiber, 12 mg cholesterol, 100 mg sodium; 17 percent of calories from fat.

Wonderful Strawberry Waffles

EQUIPMENT

food processor or blender

electric waffle iron

mixing bowl

measuring cups

measuring spoons

mixing spoon

INGREDIENTS

1 cup sliced strawberries

2 cups Bisquick reduced-fat baking mix

1⅓ cups low-fat milk

1 egg

2 teaspoons strawberry extract

10 drops red food coloring

Canola oil nonstick cooking spray

Light dessert topping or canned light whipped cream (optional)

GROWN-UP PREP

1. Put strawberries in food processor or blender and pulse until chopped into very small pieces (not pureed).

2. Turn on waffle iron about 5 minutes before Cooking Time.

1. Your child can measure Bisquick and put it in mixing bowl.

2. Your child can measure the milk and add it to the Bisquick.

3. Your child can crack the egg and add it to the Bisquick.

4. Stir ingredients. While you are stirring up this mixture, your child can measure strawberry extract and add it to the mixture.

5. Your child can count to 10 as he or she gently adds the red food coloring to the waffle batter.

6. Once batter is blended well, you or your child can stir in the strawberry pieces.

7. Coat waffle iron (top and bottom) lightly with nonstick cooking spray. Measure the amount of batter recommended by the manufacturer for that particular waffle iron and pour it onto the hot waffle iron. Bake until steaming stops. Repeat until all batter is used.

Serve with dessert topping or whipped cream, if desired.

Makes 12 4-inch waffles

Per waffle: 100 calories, 3 g protein, 16 g carbohydrate, 2 g fat, .5 g fiber, 20 mg cholesterol, 248 mg sodium; 20 percent of calories from fat.

Wonderful Chocolate Waffles

EQUIPMENT

stove

medium-sized saucepan

electric waffle iron

mixing bowl

measuring cups

measuring spoons

mixing spoon

INGREDIENTS

3 tablespoons butter or margarine

2 squares unsweetened baking chocolate

$\frac{1}{3}$ cup sugar

$\frac{1}{3}$ cup light corn syrup

$1\frac{1}{2}$ teaspoons vanilla extract

1 egg

$\frac{1}{4}$ cup egg substitute

$1\frac{1}{2}$ cups all-purpose flour

1 teaspoon cream of tartar

$\frac{1}{2}$ teaspoon baking soda

$\frac{1}{2}$ cup low-fat buttermilk

Canola oil nonstick cooking spray

CLASSROOM HINT

If you want to melt the butter and chocolate in front of class, use a hot plate and a medium-sized nonstick saucepan.

GROWN-UP PREP

Turn on waffle iron about 5 minutes before Cooking Time.

COOKING TIME

1. Your child can help you measure the butter and chocolate and place in medium-sized saucepan. Melt the mixture over low heat.

2. Your child can measure the sugar and corn syrup and pour them into the mixture in saucepan.

3. Your child can measure the vanilla and add it to the chocolate in the saucepan. You or your child can stir the mixture. Once blended, remove from heat.

4. Add egg, then beat mixture until blended well. Add egg substitute and beat until blended.

5. Your child can measure the flour, cream of tartar, and baking soda and put them in the mixing bowl. Stir together with spoon.

6. Pour the chocolate mixture into the mixing bowl with flour mixture; add the buttermilk. Stir until blended well.

7. Coat waffle iron with nonstick cooking spray. Pour in the amount of batter recommended by the waffle iron manufacturer. Remove waffle when done (the waffle will become nice and crisp as it cools).

Makes 12 4- or 5-inch waffles

Per waffle: 167 calories, 3.5 g protein, 26.5 g carbohydrate, 6 g fat, 1 g fiber, 25 mg cholesterol, 118 mg sodium; 32 percent of calories from fat.

▶ X-Tra Super Salsa

EQUIPMENT

plastic knives

blender or food processor

cheese grater

measuring spoons

can opener

INGREDIENTS

2 medium-sized tomatoes

½ small mild or sweet onion

3 tablespoons diced green chilies

1 tablespoon distilled white vinegar

Fresh cilantro

⅛ teaspoon salt

1 clove garlic, pressed or minced

Black pepper

8 cups reduced-fat tortilla chips (optional)

COOKING TIME

1. Your child can wash the tomatoes well. Show your child how to dice the tomatoes using plastic knife. Put in blender or food processor.

2. Help your child grate the onion. Put onion in blender or food processor.

3. Help your child open canned chilies with can opener, measure, and add to onions.

4. Your child can measure vinegar and add to chilies.

5. Show your child how to tear the cilantro leaves from the bunch and wash them well. Chop cilantro with plastic knife, measure 1½ tablespoons, and add to chilies.

6. Measure salt and add to chilies along with garlic and black pepper to taste.

7. Blend or process briefly until blended.

Serve with reduced-fat tortilla chips, if desired.

Makes about 2½ cups of salsa

Per ¼-cup serving: 15 calories, .6 g protein, 3.4 g carbohydrate, .15 g fat, 1 g fiber, 0 mg cholesterol, 50 mg sodium; 8 percent of calories from fat.

Your-Favorite-Fruit-Flavored Frozen Yogurt

EQUIPMENT

ice-cream maker

plastic knife

food processor or potato masher

electric mixer and mixing bowl

measuring cups

measuring spoons

spoon or rubber spatula

can opener

INGREDIENTS

Fresh or frozen fruit of your favorite kind

2 cups low-fat yogurt of your favorite fruit flavor

1 14-ounce can fat-free sweetened condensed skimmed milk

1 cup whole or low-fat milk

1 tablespoon vanilla extract

1 tablespoon extract of your favorite fruit flavor

GROWN-UP PREP

At least a day ahead of time, freeze portion of ice-cream maker that needs to be frozen if using electric ice-cream maker. Consult owner's manual if you have questions.

COOKING TIME

1. Prepare fruit (wash, remove stems, slice, and so forth); then puree in food processor or with potato masher. Place 1½ cups in mixing bowl.

2. Have your child add the yogurt to the pureed fruit using a spoon.

3. Open the sweetened condensed milk can and help your child pour it into the mixing bowl, scraping the inside of can carefully with spoon. Your child can measure the milk, vanilla, and fruit extract and add them to the condensed milk.

4. Blend ingredients well with mixer. Pour into ice-cream maker.

5. Continue to make frozen yogurt following ice-cream maker manufacturer's directons.

NOTE: This recipe was tested using an electric ice-cream maker.

Makes about 7 cups of frozen yogurt

Per ½-cup serving: 133 calories, 4.5 g protein, 26.5 g carbohydrate, 1 g fat, .5 g fiber, 5 mg cholesterol, 58 mg sodium; 7 percent of calories from fat.

▶ Yummy Cheese Toast

GROWN-UP PREP

Process shredded Parmesan cheese into smaller pieces in small food processor; put in shallow container and set aside.

COOKING TIME

1. Help your child measure and put diet margarine in small bowl. Help your child use garlic press to press garlic; add to margarine.

2. Show your older child how to melt the butter in microwave oven (or use stove) and add to diet margarine. Stir margarine mixture well.

3. Using a plastic knife or small spoon, your child can spread some of the mixture on one side of a slice of the Texas toast bread.

4. Press the buttered side of the bread down into the bowl of Parmesan cheese. Press gently to coat surface with the cheese.

5. Heat nonstick frying pan over medium-low heat. Spray buttered side of bread lightly with nonstick cooking spray and lay bread buttered side down in the pan. Spray top of bread with nonstick cooking spray. If you can fit two slices of bread in the pan, repeat with other slice.

6. After bottom sides are browned, about 1 minute, flip slices over with spatula and let other sides brown. Remove slices from pan. Sprinkle lightly with paprika to taste, if desired. An adult can cut each slice into two triangles or three strips, if desired.

7. Repeat with remaining bread.

Makes 5 slices

Per slice: 195 calories, 7 g protein, 25 g carbohydrate, 7.5 g fat, 1 g fiber, 11 mg cholesterol, 394 mg sodium; 34 percent of calories from fat.

Zucchini Sticks

EQUIPMENT

knife

oven

cookie sheets

garlic press

spoon

measuring cups

measuring spoons

food processor, blender, or electric
  mixer and small bowl

2 shallow bowls

INGREDIENTS

4 medium-sized zucchini

Canola oil nonstick cooking spray

2 garlic cloves

⅓ cup egg substitute

1 tablespoon mayonnaise

½ cup Italian-style breadcrumbs

GROWN-UP PREP

1. Wash and dry zucchini. Cut in half lengthwise. Then cut each of these halves in half and continue until you have 32 pieces.

2. Preheat oven to 400°F.

COOKING TIME

1. Coat cookie sheets generously with nonstick cooking spray.

2. Have your child put garlic cloves in garlic press. Your child can squeeze the garlic press handles together to press the garlic out. Use a spoon to scrape the garlic off the press.

3. Your child can measure the egg substitute and mayonnaise and put them along with the garlic in food processor, blender, or small bowl. Blend the mixture well and then put it in a shallow bowl.

4. Put the breadcrumbs in the other shallow bowl.

5. Your child can dip the zucchini sticks into the egg mixture first and the breadcrumbs mixture next. Place on prepared cookie sheets.

6. You or your child can spray the tops of the zucchini sticks with nonstick cooking spray. Bake in center of oven for 12 minutes.

Makes about 32 Zucchini Sticks

Per 4-stick serving: 65 calories, 3 g protein, 9.5 g carbohydrate, 2 g fat, 1.3 g fiber, 1 mg cholesterol, 278 mg sodium; 26 percent of calories from fat.

Zebra Pudding Cups

Z

EQUIPMENT

salad bowls

2-cup measure

electric mixer and mixing bowl

spatula

medium-sized bowl

measuring spoons

8 plastic cups (tumblers)

2 ¼-cup measuring cups

INGREDIENTS

Assorted White Toppings

1 cup miniature marshmallows

¼ cup flaked coconut

½ cup yogurt-covered raisins

Assorted Black Toppings

1 cup crushed reduced-fat chocolate wafers

¼ cup miniature chocolate chips

½ cup raisins or chocolate-covered raisins

2 cups low-fat milk

1 3.4-ounce package vanilla instant pudding mix

2 cups low-fat milk

1 3.4-ounce package chocolate instant pudding mix

Light dessert topping or light canned whipped cream (optional)

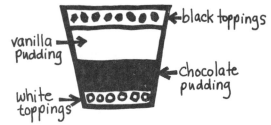

GROWN-UP PREP

Put each of the various white and black zebra toppings in its own salad bowl.

1. Have your child measure 2 cups low-fat milk; pour it into the mixing bowl.

2. Your child can tear open the envelope of vanilla pudding mix and pour it into the mixing bowl.

3. On low speed, mix the milk and pudding powder for about 2 minutes (pudding will start to thicken). Spoon the pudding into medium-sized bowl; set aside.

4. Your child can measure and pour 2 cups low-fat milk into the mixing bowl.

5. Your child can tear open the envelope of chocolate pudding mix and pour it into the mixing bowl.

6. On low speed, mix the milk and pudding powder for about 2 minutes; set aside.

7. Your child can sprinkle 1 tablespoon of any of the white toppings in the bottoms of several plastic cups.

8. Your child can use a ¼-cup measure to scoop ¼ cup of the chocolate pudding into each cup. Then your child can use a second ¼-cup measure to scoop ¼ cup of vanilla pudding into each cup.

9. Your child can sprinkle 1 tablespoon of any of the black toppings on top of the vanilla pudding in each of the cups.

10. Put a dab of light dessert topping or canned whipped cream on top, if desired.

NOTE: Your child can crush the chocolate wafers into crumbs for you. Just place the cookies in a sandwich-sized resealable plastic bag, and then your child can roll over them with a rolling pin or crush them with a toy hammer or the bottom of a jelly jar.

Makes 8 pudding cups

Per ½-cup serving (with 1 tablespoon miniature marshmallows and 1 tablespoon reduced-fat chocolate wafers): 160 calories, 4 g protein, 35 g carbohydrate, 1.5 g fat, .5 g fiber, 5 mg cholesterol, 450 mg sodium; 10 percent of calories from fat.

LONG VOWEL ACTIVITIES

Angel-in-a-Cloud Cookies

EQUIPMENT

oven

egg separator

small mixing bowl

large cookie sheet

parchment paper

measuring cups

measuring spoons

electric mixer

decorating bag fitted with a large
    star tip

wire rack

INGREDIENTS

2 egg whites

½ teaspoon vanilla extract

¼ teaspoon cream of tartar

½ cup sugar

Assorted decorations such as
    rainbow sprinkles, gumdrops, or
    Life Savers candies

GROWN-UP PREP

1. Preheat oven to 300°F.

2. Set egg whites in small mixing bowl and let stand at room temperature for
   30 minutes.

3. Line large cookie sheet with parchment paper.

COOKING TIME

1. Your child can measure the vanilla and cream of tartar and add them to the egg whites. Beat with an electric mixer on medium speed until soft peaks form (tips curl).

2. Your child can measure the sugar. Have your child gradually add the sugar to the egg whites, 1 tablespoon at a time, beating on high speed until stiff peaks form (tips stand straight), and sugar is almost dissolved.

3. Spoon meringue into decorating bag fitted with a large star tip (½-inch opening). You and your child can pipe 1½-inch-diameter stars about 1½ inches apart onto prepared cookie sheet.

4. Your child can press a gumdrop or Life Savers into the center of each star or place rainbow sprinkles over the top.

5. Bake for about 15 minutes or until cookies just start to turn brown. Turn off oven and let cookies dry in oven (keep door closed) for 15 minutes. Remove cookies and cool on wire rack.

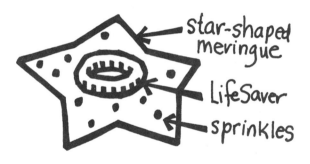

Makes about 20 large cookies

Per cookie: 21 calories, .4 g protein, 5 g carbohydrate, 0 g fat, 0 mg cholesterol, 6 mg sodium; 0 percent of calories from fat.

Easy Mexican Pizza

EQUIPMENT

nonstick frying pan

stove

spatula

measuring cups

cheese grater

bowl

nonstick electric skillet

measuring spoons

INGREDIENTS

Canola oil nonstick cooking spray

½ pound superlean ground beef

¼ to ½ envelope Lawry's taco seasoning

⅓ cup water

3 ounces reduced-fat Monterey Jack cheese

3 ounces reduced-fat sharp cheddar cheese

8 flour tortillas

½ cup mild salsa

GROWN-UP PREP

Coat nonstick frying pan with nonstick cooking spray. Add ground beef and brown over medium heat, crumbling it into small pieces as it cooks. Sprinkle taco seasoning over the top along with water. Stir well and let cook a couple of minutes until water has evaporated. Turn off heat and set seasoned beef aside.

COOKING TIME

1. Help your child grate the Monterey Jack cheese and the cheddar cheese and toss in bowl to mix well.

2. Coat nonstick electric skillet with cooking spray and heat pan to medium-low. Add one flour tortilla to pan and spoon ¼ of the beef mixture evenly over the tortilla. Sprinkle about ⅓ cup of the grated cheese over the meat. Spoon about 2 tablespoons of the salsa evenly over the cheese. Top with another tortilla and spray the top with nonstick cooking spray.

3. By now the underside of the bottom tortilla should be lightly browned. Carefully flip the Mexican pizza over with the spatula and lightly brown other side.

4. Repeat process with remaining ingredients.

Makes 4 Mexican pizzas

Per Mexican pizza: 416 calories, 25.5 g protein, 42 g carbohydrate, 15.7 g fat, 2 g fiber, 40 mg cholesterol, 684 mg sodium; 34 percent of calories from fat.

▶ Ice Cream

EQUIPMENT

ice-cream maker

electric mixer and mixing bowl

storage-sized resealable plastic bag

toy hammer

mixing spoon

INGREDIENTS

1½ cups whole milk

1 14-ounce can fat-free sweetened
   condensed milk

⅓ cup chocolate syrup

9 to 12 reduced-fat chocolate
   sandwich cookies

GROWN-UP PREP

Prepare ice-cream maker according to manufacturer's directions. I need to freeze the container of my electric ice-cream maker at least one day ahead.

1. In mixing bowl, beat milk with sweetened condensed milk and chocolate syrup until combined.

2. Pour mixture into ice-cream maker and continue, following ice-cream maker manufacturer's directions.

3. While you are all waiting for the ice-cream maker to work its magic, put the cookies in a storage-sized resealable plastic bag and let your child crush them into pieces with a toy hammer.

4. Once ice cream is ready (frozen and fluffy), stir the cookie pieces in by hand.

Makes about 4 cups of Ice Cream

Per ½-cup serving: 260 calories, 6.5 g protein, 47 g carbohydrate, 5 g fat, 10.5 mg cholesterol, 165 mg sodium; 17 percent of calories from fat.

Oh-Boy Orange Balls

EQUIPMENT

measuring cups

shallow dishes

zesting tool

measuring spoons

sharp knife

large food processor

INGREDIENTS

$\frac{3}{4}$ cup powdered sugar

$\frac{3}{4}$ cup unsweetened cocoa

1 to 2 oranges

1 11- or 12-ounce box reduced-fat
  vanilla wafers

$\frac{3}{4}$ cup powdered sugar

$\frac{1}{4}$ cup unsweetened cocoa

$1\frac{1}{2}$ cups pecan pieces or other nuts

3 tablespoons light corn syrup

GROWN-UP PREP

Put $\frac{3}{4}$ cup powdered sugar in a shallow dish. Put $\frac{3}{4}$ cup cocoa in a second shallow dish.

1. Start your child using the zesting tool on the oranges to grate zest from the orange peel. Once 2 teaspoons have been collected, finely chop the grated peel with a sharp knife; set aside.

2. Your child can put the entire box of vanilla wafers in the food processor. Process until fine crumbs are made.

3. Your child can measure the ¾ cup powdered sugar and add it to the cookie crumbs.

4. Your child can measure and add ¼ cup cocoa and pecan pieces to the cookie crumbs.

5. Measure and add the light corn syrup to the cookie crumbs (it can get a bit sticky).

6. Cut the oranges in halves. Then, your child can squeeze the orange halves to extract ½ cup of orange juice; pour the juice into the food processor.

7. Pulse the food processor until a soft dough is formed. Add 1 tablespoon more orange juice if the mixture is too dry.

8. Your child can grab enough dough to make a 1-inch ball. Have your child shape it into a ball by rolling it between his or her hands. Now your child can roll the balls in the powdered sugar or cocoa in shallow dishes.

Makes about 48 balls

Per 2 balls: 133 calories, 1.3 g protein, 19.5 g carbohydrate, 6 g fat, 1 g fiber, 0 mg cholesterol, 56 mg sodium; 40 percent of calories from fat.

Uniform Corn Cakes

EQUIPMENT

oven

8-inch-square pan

measuring cups

measuring spoons

small mixing bowl

electric mixer

large mixing bowl

foil

ice-cream scoop or cookie scoop

INGREDIENTS

Canola oil nonstick cooking spray

3 tablespoons butter, softened

¼ cup corn syrup

½ cup masa

3 tablespoons cold water

3 tablespoons cornmeal

2 tablespoons sugar

2 tablespoons milk

¼ teaspoon baking powder

¼ teaspoon salt

10 ounces frozen corn kernels

GROWN-UP PREP

Preheat oven to 350°F. Coat 8-inch-square baking pan with nonstick cooking spray.

COOKING TIME

1. Your child can measure the butter and corn syrup and put them in small mixing bowl; beat until fluffy and creamy.

2. Your child can measure the masa and add it gradually to the butter mixture.

3. Your child can measure the water and add it gradually to the butter mixture.

4. Your child can measure the cornmeal, sugar, milk, baking powder, and salt and put them in large mixing bowl. Mix quickly, and then add the butter mixture and corn kernels; beat briefly.

5. Pour batter into prepared baking pan. Cover with foil and bake 40 minutes or until corn cake has a firm texture. Let cool 15 minutes.

6. Your child can use a small ice-cream scoop or cookie scoop to scoop out round cakes, or your child can cut out square corn cakes by cutting 4 columns across and 4 columns down.

NOTE: *Masa harina* is "corn masa mix," similar to cornmeal except the corn is treated with lime water and specially ground. It is typically used to make tortillas and tamales. It is available in large supermarkets' ethnic foods sections. Quaker Oats is one brand of *masa harina*.

Makes 16 squares

Per square: 70 calories, 1 g protein, 12 g carbohydrate, 2.4 g fat, 1 g fiber, 6 mg cholesterol, 70 mg sodium; 29 percent of calories from fat.

ALPHABET LUNCH BOX

Children love finding something different in their otherwise predictable lunch boxes. Sandwiches turn into something fun when they are shaped into letters of the alphabet. Later you can ask your child what words she spelled at lunch with her sandwich letters. My daughter especially liked reading her secret message, which I hid in her cored apple. Even her friends looked forward to reading what I wrote each day. As her reading ability grew so did the length of my messages.

▶ Alphabet Sandwiches

EQUIPMENT

small bowl

can opener

measuring spoon

plastic knives or serrated knife

plastic sandwich bag

INGREDIENTS

6 slices sandwich bread

Ham and Cheese

3 ounces (3 to 6 slices) lean ham
slices

3 reduced-fat cheese slices
(3 ounces)

1 tablespoon low-fat or light
mayonnaise or prepared mustard

Peanut Butter and Jelly

6 tablespoons reduced-fat peanut
butter

3 to 5 tablespoons reduced-sugar
jelly

Tuna Salad

1 6½-ounce can solid white tuna in
water

2 to 3 tablespoons low-fat or light
mayonnaise

⅓ cup diced celery

1 tablespoon minced onion

1 tablespoon pickle relish

⅛ teaspoon pepper

Prepare desired sandwich filling. If making tuna salad, just blend ingredients in a small bowl.

COOKING TIME

1. You and your child can use plastic knives or you can use a serrated knife to cut bread slices into letter shapes. Make two of each letter. You may be able to get two letters out of 1 slice of bread. For example, 1 slice can be cut into an *L* and a *T*. Experiment to find other combinations of letters.

2. Spread the sandwich filling on top of one of the letters, and then place the matching letter on top to make a sandwich. For peanut butter and jelly, spread the peanut butter on top of one letter and the jelly on the matching letter, and then put them together to make a sandwich. For ham and cheese, place the bread letter on top of a slice of ham and cheese. Trace the bread letter with a plastic knife. Spread mayonnaise or mustard on one of the bread letters, and then piece the ham and cheese slices together to make a sandwich.

3. Place sandwich letters in sandwich bags and put in lunch box.

   If you were able to make two letter sandwiches for every two pieces of bread, you should have 6 letter sandwiches to play with. Your child can spell out words with these letters. For example, with the letter sandwiches *I, L, O, V, E,* and *U,* you can spell out *I LOVE U.*

Makes 3 sandwiches

Per 3 ham-and-cheese letter sandwiches: 388 calories, 26.5 g protein, 40 g carbohydrate, 13.8 g fat, 4.5 g fiber, 44 mg cholesterol, 1,276 mg sodium; 32 percent of calories from fat.

Per 3 peanut-butter-and-jelly letter sandwiches: 547 calories, 77 g carbohydrate, 20 g fat, 8 g fiber, 0 mg cholesterol, 781 mg sodium; 33 percent of calories from fat.

Per 3 tuna-salad letter sandwiches: 335 calories, 43 g carbohydrate, 6.5 g fat, 5 g fiber, 27 mg cholesterol, 817 mg sodium; 18 percent of calories from fat.

Secret Message Fruit

When your child takes the fruit out of his or her lunch box at lunchtime, he or she will open up the fruit and find a secret message inside to read!

EQUIPMENT

slip of paper

pen (or other writing instrument)

sandwich-sized resealable plastic bag
   or plastic wrap

knife or apple corer

plastic wrap or aluminum foil

INGREDIENTS

1 apple or orange

GROWN-UP PREP

1. Write a secret message (appropriate for your child's reading level) on a slip of paper. Put the slip of paper in a resealable plastic bag, pushing out air, or fold neatly in plastic wrap.

2. Use an apple cutter or knife to core and slice an apple in wedges, or use a knife to cut an orange into 6 wedges, removing fibrous white center with your fingers.

3. Piece the apple or orange wedges together (reforming the fruit) with the secret message on the inside. Wrap the fruit with plastic wrap or foil.

Makes 1 Secret Message Fruit

Per apple: 125 calories, .4 g protein, 32.5 g carbohydrate, .8 g fat, 4 g fiber, 0 mg cholesterol, 0 mg sodium; 5 percent of calories from fat.

Per orange: 64 calories, 1.5 g protein, 16 g carbohydrate, .1 g fat, 2.3 g fiber, 0 mg cholesterol, 1 mg sodium; 2 percent of calories from fat.

ALPHABET PARTIES

Learning the alphabet is a milestone for your growing child. Celebrate this landmark in learning with one or all of these fun alphabet party activities.

▶ Alphabet Petits Fours

EQUIPMENT

oven

15½" × 10½" jelly roll pan

waxed paper

electric mixer and mixing bowl

wire rack

measuring cups

measuring spoons

1-quart saucepan

knife

small mixing bowl

small spoons

frosting tube with writing tip

INGREDIENTS

Canola oil nonstick cooking spray

White Cake Petits Fours

1 box white cake mix, such as Betty
    Crocker SuperMoist

⅓ cup nonfat sour cream

1¼ cups water

3 egg whites

⅔ cup reduced-sugar strawberry,
    grape, or apple jelly

Chocolate Fudge Petits Fours

1 box devil's food cake mix, such as
    Pillsbury Moist Supreme

½ cup nonfat sour cream

1¼ cups water

¾ cup egg substitute or 3 egg whites

⅔ cup microwavable hot fudge
    topping

Sugar Icing

1 16-ounce package powdered sugar

5 tablespoons water

1 teaspoon almond extract

Tube frosting in assorted colors

GROWN-UP PREP

Select which type of petits fours you want to prepare, white cake or chocolate fudge. The directions will be basically the same.

1. Preheat oven to 350°F. Coat jelly roll pan with nonstick cooking spray; line with waxed paper. Spray waxed paper with nonstick cooking spray.

2. Prepare cake mix according to directions but substituting nonfat sour cream for the oil and 3 egg whites for the eggs. Spread batter in prepared pan.

3. Bake cake about 20 minutes or until center springs back when touched lightly. Cool on wire rack 10 minutes. Invert cake from pan onto rack; peel off paper and cool completely.

COOKING TIME

1. In saucepan over low heat, melt jelly or hot fudge. (Your child can help stir if age appropriate.) Your child can glaze the cake with the mixture using a spoon.

2. Cut lengthwise into six strips. Then cut each strip crosswise into 9 or 10 pieces. Your child can now count the 54 or 60 pieces.

CLASSROOM HINTS

This is a wonderful treat for the classroom. You can do it a couple of ways. You can make the petits fours at home, stopping after letting the icing dry, and then bring them into the classroom for the students to decorate with their favorite letters of the alphabet. You'll need to have several tubes of frosting available for them to decorate the cakes with. Or you can make the petits fours at home, stopping before drizzling them with icing. You can set up several wire racks in the classroom and let the students drizzle the icing on their own two or three petits fours. Let the petits fours dry during the school day, and the students can decorate them with the alphabet letters after the cakes have dried.

3. Arrange half of the squares 1 inch apart on the wire rack over some waxed paper.

4. You and your child can blend the icing ingredients together in a small mixing bowl; beat until smooth.

5. You and your child can drizzle the icing over the glazed squares (to cover the tops and sides) using small spoons. Return dripped icing to the bowl from waxed paper, and beat smooth to reuse, adding ½ teaspoon water if necessary.

6. When icing is dry, decorate the tops of the iced cakes with tube frosting (using the writing tip), marking each cake with different letters of the alphabet. Since there are at least 54 cakes and 26 letters in the alphabet, you will have two of every letter.

7. Your child can make words by putting different letters together.

NOTE: If preparation time is limited, skip making the cakes and use Entenmann's Fat Free Golden or Chocolate Loaf instead. Freeze the loaves so they will be easier to slice into petits fours cakes.

Makes at least 54 petits fours

Per 2 white cake with jelly filling petits fours: 162 calories, 1.3 g protein, 36 g carbohydrate, 1.3 g fat, 0 mg cholesterol, 131 mg sodium; 7 percent of calories from fat.

Per 2 chocolate cake with fudge filling petits fours: 180 calories, 2.3 g protein, 37 g carbohydrate, 2.3 g fat, 0 mg cholesterol, 171 mg sodium; 11 percent of calories from fat.

Alphabet Snack Mix

GROWN-UP PREP

This is a terrific group or party activity. You write each letter of the alphabet on a slip of paper and put the slips of paper into a hat. Have each child draw a slip of paper. Then each child brings in a snack food that begins with the letter he or she drew. For example, a child who has *A* can bring a cup of dried apples, a child who has *B* can bring a cup of bagel chips, and a child who has *J* can bring a cup of Cracker Jack or jelly beans. For the more difficult letters, just have the child bring in a food with his or her letter somewhere in the name of that food. If you have fewer than 26 children in your group, just leave the last few letters out.

When it is time for the party, each child can put his or her food into the punch bowl, telling the class which letter of the alphabet he or she drew. After all the snacks have been put in the bowl, mix it up well. Then fill paper bowls or cups with a sampling of the mixture.

EQUIPMENT

slips of paper

pen

hat

punch bowl

salad bowl spoons

paper bowls or paper cups

INGREDIENTS

Assorted snack mix ingredients

COOKING TIME

1. Ask the class, "Who pulled the letter *A* from the hat?" and so forth. The students can now add their snack items to the punch bowl, telling the class the name of each food.

2. After all the students have added their alphabet snack food to the punch bowl, mix it up with salad bowl spoons. Add some to each of the bowls or cups, and the students can enjoy their alphabet snack!

Alphabet Pizza

This is a great activity to do for a family dinner in celebration of your child's learning to write the entire alphabet.

EQUIPMENT

pizza pan or cookie sheet
oven
rolling pin
large spoon
plastic knife

INGREDIENTS

Canola oil nonstick cooking spray

Flour

Pizza dough (see Index for Italian Breadsticks recipe) or packaged Italian bread shells

1 cup bottled pizza sauce or marinara sauce

Pizza Toppings

3 to 4 ounces American or cheddar cheese slices

3 to 4 ounces part-skim mozzarella cheese, sliced thin

2 Roma tomatoes

1 zucchini

10 less-fat salami slices *or* 15 less-fat turkey pepperoni slices

GROWN-UP PREP

1. Spray pizza pan or cookie sheet with nonstick cooking spray.
2. Preheat oven to 400°F.

COOKING TIME

1. If using the pizza dough, your child can help you roll the dough out on a lightly floured surface with a rolling pin. You and your child can use your hands to stretch the dough, too. Place dough or shell on pizza pan or cookie sheet.
2. Your child can spread the pizza or marinara sauce over the pizza crust using a large spoon.
3. Help your child create letters out of the pizza toppings to put on the pizza using plastic knife. For example, your child can cut the slices of cheddar and mozzarella cheese into strips and use longer and shorter ½-inch-wide strips to make straight letters: *A, E, F, L, M, N, V, X, H, I, T, W, Y,* and *Z.* The cheese slices can also be cut into some of the more difficult letter shapes: *G, J, K, P, R,* and *S.* Your child can cut the tomato, zucchini, and salami or pepperoni slices into the letters that can easily be shaped by cutting off of a circle: *O, Q, U, C, D* (and two *D*s can make *B*).
4. Top your prepared pizza crust with the cheese letters first, then the vegetable letters, and then the meat letters.
5. Bake pizza in oven until crust is lightly browned and cheese is bubbling, 10 to 15 minutes.

Makes 1 large pizza, about 5 servings

Per ⅕-pizza serving (with a pizza of 1 10-ounce Italian bread shell, 1 cup marinara sauce, 6 ounces of reduced-fat cheese, 2 Roma tomatoes, and 1 cup of zucchini slices): 320 calories, 20 g protein, 35 g carbohydrate, 11.5 g fat, 1.5 g fiber, 24 mg cholesterol, 937 mg sodium; 32 percent of calories from fat.

Index

S